FIGHTING THE BATTLES OF AMERICA

Books by Daniel McDonald Johnson

This Cursed War: Lachlan McIntosh of Georgia and the Tribulations of his Family during the American Revolution

Savannah, Augusta & Brier Creek: The Conquest of Georgia in the American Revolution

Mr. McIntosh's Family: The Mackintosh Clan and the McIntosh Family in the Jacobite Risings, the Settlement of Darien, Georgia, and the Struggle for the Colonial American Southern Frontier

Fort Morris Battleground: An Illustrated Guide to a Revolutionary War Site at Sunbury, Georgia

FIGHTING THE BATTLES OF AMERICA

John McIntosh in the American Revolution, East Florida Rebellions, and War of 1812

Daniel McDonald Johnson

Copyright 2022

Independently published by
Daniel McDonald Johnson
Post Office Box 747
Allendale, South Carolina 29810

Distributed by Ingram Book Company

ISBN: 978-0-578-28047-9

About the Cover

The image on the cover is a photograph that has been edited to resemble a watercolor painting. The model holding the sword is Bill Elder of Deland, Florida. He portrayed George Washington during an event at Fort Morris State Historic Site on November 22, 2014. I asked him to let me photograph his sword to illustrate the historical event when the Georgia legislature honored the gallantry of John McIntosh by presenting him a sword engraved with the words "Come and Take It."

Daniel McDonald Johnson

Contents

Hero of the American Revolution   3

Rebel in Spanish East Florida   37

General in the War of 1812   77

Biographical Information   95

A Body in Motion   101

Photographs   103

Notes   115

Bibliography   143

Index   151

FIGHTING THE BATTLES OF AMERICA

Hero of the American Revolution

JOHN MCINTOSH SET OFF on an expedition. As a lieutenant colonel commanding the 3rd Georgia Battalion of Continental troops in the third year of the American Revolution, he participated in the third invasion of British East Florida.[1] The Georgia Continentals marched southward to the Altamaha River and arrived on April 14, 1778, at the ruins of Fort Howe, where they planned to rendezvous with the other bodies of troops. The invasion plan called for coordination among Georgia state troops, the Georgia navy, Continental troops from the Georgia line, Continental troops from South Carolina's 1st Regiment, 3rd Regiment and 6th Regiment, South Carolina militia, and Continental troops from the Southern Department.[2]

On April 16, Colonel Samuel Elbert led about 350 Georgia troops to Darien. The infantry went aboard three galleys, and an artillery detachment loaded two field pieces on a flatboat. The flotilla went down the Altamaha to St. Simons Island. Elbert "earnestly entreated" his officers and soldiers "to pay the strictest attention to their duty, in which case their commanding officer will insure them of success against the plunderers of their country and the common enemies of the rights of mankind."[3] While a few marines remained on the galleys, the infantry went ashore. A detachment of one hundred men entered the town of Frederica and captured several members of a British naval crew.

Early on the morning of April 19, the American galleys took aim at the enemy ships *Hitchinbrook*, *Rebecca* and *Snow*. Elbert reported to General Howe "our three little men-of-war made an attack on these three British vessels, who have spread terror on our coast, and who were drawn up in the order of battle; but the weight of our metal soon dampened their courage." After the *Hitchinbrook* and *Rebecca* ran aground and laid over at low tide, their captains "struck the British tyrant's colors and surrendered to American arms." The British sailors "took to their boats and abandoned everything on board, of which we immediately took possession. Captain Ellis, of the *Hitchinbrook*, was drowned and Captain Mowbrary, of the *Rebecca*, made his escape."[4]

Cargo on the captured ships included uniforms for South Carolina Continental troops; the uniforms previously had been captured by the British in naval action off Charleston. Elbert's victory deprived the British of control of the inland waterway and reduced British East Florida's naval force to only a single frigate.[5]

The Americans secured the captured ships at Sunbury and then made a forced march back to Fort Howe, where Elbert expected a British attack. "I know your anxiety for the safety of this state is such that no time will be lost," Elbert told Colonel John White. Elbert also asked White to arrange for rice and salt to be shipped from the coast to Fort Howe.[6]

On May 9, Major General Howe—commander of the Southern Department of the Continental forces—reached the fort on the Altamaha named in his honor.[7] Howe was delighted that Elbert had launched the campaign with a victory, and declared "how highly he approves the conduct of Colo. Elbert in the late expedition against the enemy at Frederica, and with equal pleasure applauds the spirited behavior of the officers and men, both of the galleys and of the army who were upon that command."[8]

While the Americans remained in camp, Howe approved the execution of several deserters. "Desertion is of all other crimes the greatest a soldier can be guilty of," Howe told his men. "In committing it every moral sanction is violated; the cause of freedom, the darling rights and privileges—both of the present and succeeding generations—which soldiers were ordained particular to secure and protect, are relinquished and betrayed."[9]

In late May the army moved from Fort Howe to Reid's Bluff on the south side of the Altamaha, and in early June proceeded into contested territory. Colonel Elbert issued marching orders for the Georgia brigade:

> Colo. Stirk, Lieut. Colo. Roberts & Major Lane to the 1st line, and Colo. Rae with Lieut. Colo. McIntosh to the second. No man is to be suffered to quit his rank, while on the march, and officers are strictly enjoined to keep their divisions in order for forming at a moment's warning. When the woods will not admit of marching by platoons in front they are to file by the right; should any part of the of the troops be attacked on their march, they are to maintain their guard, till the commanding officer either reinforces them or gives orders for a retreat. Each man to be furnished with 24 rounds, exclusive of the ammunition they have loose; they must have a sufficient quantity of wadding and three spare flints; the troops will be served with three days' salt provisions, and as much rice and indian meal as will last 8 days is to be transported in wagons; beeves will be drove on for the use of the army.[10]

By June 22, the Continentals had reached the south side of the Satilla River and by the end of June the army camped at the ruins of Fort Tonyn on the St. Marys River. Illness struck hundreds of soldiers, who were sent to hospitals on the Georgia coast. The soldiers remaining in camp lacked an adequate amount of tents, kettles, canteens, medicine, food and equipment.[11]

While Howe commanded the Georgia Continentals and several units of South Carolina Continentals, Georgia Governor John Houstoun maintained command of a force of Georgia militia. On June 30, a detachment of Georgia militia attacked a band of East Florida Rangers near a British outpost at Alligator Creek Bridge; more than twelve Georgians were killed and several were wounded; one British soldier was killed, and several British and loyalist soldiers were wounded.[12]

Conditions continued to deteriorate for the Continentals camped at Fort Tonyn. Because provisions were resupplied sporadically, the men ran out of rice and went for three days without bread.[13]

General Howe convened a council of war for the Continental officers, including John McIntosh. Howe pointed out what their expedition had accomplished so far: driving the British out of Georgia, and destroying the British advance post at Fort Tonyn. Howe also pointed out the obstacles facing the expedition: divided command between the Continentals and the state militia; impassable roads for the infantry; insufficient horses; unhealthy climate conditions; an elusive enemy withdrawing to the far side of the St. Johns River; impassable narrows for the galleys and an inferior naval force compared to the British flotilla. The council voted unanimously to abandon the expedition.[14] On July 14, about two months after he arrived on the Georgia-Florida frontier, Howe departed from Fort Tonyn. He praised the "the cheerfulness with which the men supported a long and fatiguing march under a variety of unavoidable yet distressing circumstances."[15]

Elbert directed an evacuation at Cumberland Island. "The whole of the troops are to be embarked by low water," Elbert ordered on July 17, "that the fleet may be ready to sail with the first of the flood."[16]

The 1778 invasion of East Florida, like the previous attempts, had ended ignominiously. The most significant consequence was that Georgia forces were so weakened that they were vulnerable to British attack.

IN THE AUTUMN OF 1778, Major Mark Prevost led British troops from East Florida toward Georgia by land, and Lieutenant Colonel L.V. Fuser sailed up the waterway with additional troops. Not knowing that the British came primarily to gather provisions, Colonel Samuel Elbert prepared to defend Georgia against an all-out invasion. Elbert set up a command post at the Great Ogeechee crossing, fortified the position and awaited the British invaders.[17]

Prevost's force entered Georgia on November 19, destroying plantations, confiscating property, and taking all able-bodied men prisoner. Local militia skirmished with Prevost at Bulltown Swamp and at Riceboro Bridge but could not stop his advance.

The responsibility of countering the British invasion fell on Colonel John White, who commanded the Continental troops at Sunbury and several detachments in South Georgia. When White set out to stop Prevost, Lieutenant Colonel John McIntosh assumed command at Sunbury. White marched about a hundred men with two pieces of artillery to intercept Prevost at Midway. White's men hurriedly constructed a breastwork across the road. When General James Screven with twenty militiamen joined White at Midway, the combined force relocated to a stronger defensive position a mile and a half below Midway. Soon afterward, the British force under

Prevost arrived and a battle began. During the fighting, General Screven suffered a fatal wound. When Colonel Prevost's horse was shot from under him, the Americans thought they would win the battle, but Prevost mounted another horse and continued to press the attack. White retreated several miles past Midway toward Elbert's command post.

A British scouting party sent to Sunbury reported to Prevost that Colonel Fuser's force had not yet arrived. Prevost, considering his own lack of reinforcements and White's prospect of reinforcements from Elbert, decided to return to St. Augustine. On the way back, Prevost's men burned the church known as the Midway Meeting House and burned all homes and barns in the area. The men plundered the plantations and took all the valuable items they could carry.[18]

Storms and headwinds prevented Fuser's naval force from arriving in time to assist Prevost's land force. While Prevost's troops were leaving Midway, the armed brig *Lord George Germaine,* the privateer brig *Spitfire,* the sloop *Governor Tonyn's Revenge,* and the armed flatboat *Thunderer* approached the Georgia coast. Fuser landed 250 men on Colonel's Island, seven miles from Sunbury. Leaving a guard on the shore, he marched toward Sunbury with a grenadier company and a light infantry company of the 4th Battalion of the 60th (Royal American) Regiment of Foot, totaling 180 men. Two swivel guns mounted on a carriage provided artillery capability.

Fuser occupied the town of Sunbury during the night, an easy feat because all but five of the residents had fled to Fort Morris on the outskirts of the town. The Americans in Fort Morris detected the presence of the British in town when campfires flickered in the darkness. American gunners fired eighteen-pounders at the campfires without inflicting any casualties, because the British troops had occupied houses instead of camping outside.[19] Early the next morning, November 25, Fuser sent a letter to McIntosh saying:

> You cannot be ignorant that four armies are in motion to reduce this Province. One is already under the guns of your fort, and may be joined when I think proper by Colonel[20] Prevost who is now at the Medway [Midway] meetinghouse. The resistance you can or intend to make, will only bring destruction upon this country. On the contrary, if you will deliver me the fort which you command, lay down your arms, and remain neuter until the fate of America is determined, you shall, as well as all the inhabitants of this parish, remain in peaceable possession of your property. Your answer, which I expect in an hour's time, will determine the fate of this country, whether it is to be laid in ashes, or remain as above proposed.[21]

Inside Fort Morris, Lieutenant Colonel John McIntosh commanded 127 Continental troops of the 2nd Georgia Battalion as well as some South Carolina militiamen and residents of Sunbury, for a total of 197 men. In reply to Fuser's demand, McIntosh declared:

> We acknowledge we are not ignorant that your army is in motion to endeavor to reduce this State. We believe it entirely chimerical that Colonel Prevost is at the Meeting-House: but should it be so, we are in no degree apprehensive of danger from a junction of his army with yours. We have no property compared with the object we contend for that

we value as such a rush: —and would rather perish in a vigorous defense than accept of your proposals. We, sir, are fighting the battles of America, and therefore disdain to remain neutral till its fate is determined. As to surrendering the fort, receive this laconic reply: "COME AND TAKE IT."[22]

Fuser maintained the siege while awaiting reports of Prevost's activities. When Fuser learned that Prevost was returning to St. Augustine, he called off the siege and sailed back to Florida.

McIntosh's exploits at Sunbury not only prompted the Georgia legislature to present him a sword engraved with the words "Come and Take It"[23] but also inspired a local legend:

Lieutenant Colonel John McIntosh looked out from the parapet and saw an old man strutting outside the walls of Fort Morris at Sunbury, Georgia. The old man wore a British uniform and brandished a claymore, a huge sword favored by warriors from the Scottish Highlands. McIntosh recognized the man. They were relatives and, before the American Revolution, they had lived on neighboring plantations. The old man was Roderick McIntosh, called Rory, and he was obviously drunk.

"Surrender, you miscreants!" Rory demanded. "How dare you presume to resist his Majesty's arms?"

John told his men not to shoot. Trying to get Rory out of harm's way, John opened the gate to the fort and said, "Walk in, Mr. McIntosh, and take possession."

"No," Rory said. "I will not trust myself among such vermin, but I order you to surrender."

Someone shot at Rory, and the ball passed through his face under his eyes. He stumbled and fell, but quickly stood up. He put his hand to one cheek, looked at the blood on his hand, and then raised his hand to the other cheek and discovered that it also was covered in blood. He backed away from the fort, flourishing his sword. Several more shots rang out. Someone shouted, "Run, they'll kill you!"

Rory replied, "I come from a people who never run."

Continuing to face the enemy and still flourishing his sword, Rory stepped backward into the safety of the British lines.[24]

Like most legends, that one may be partly true. John and Rory McIntosh were kinsmen and former neighbors; John was the Continental commander at Fort Morris during the siege of 1778; Rory was a captain in the 60th Regiment of the British army at St. Augustine; and Rory was present at Fort Morris at least once during the war. The historical record, however, does not show that John and Rory were at Sunbury at the same time; Rory suffered a wound to his face during the second siege of Sunbury in January of 1779.[25]

A FLEET of at least twenty warships and troop transports set sail on November 26, 1778, to carry eight British battalions from New York to the coast of Georgia. On December 23, the fleet came to anchor off Ossabaw Island, about twenty miles from the mouth of the Savannah River. The next day the fleet entered the river.

Major General Robert Howe—a North Carolinian who had remained in Savannah after being replaced as commander of the Southern Department headquartered in Charleston—held overall command over American forces in Georgia. Colonel Samuel

Elbert—commander of the Georgia Continental forces—expected the British to come ashore at Brewton's Hill, a plantation belonging to John Girardeau. Elbert advised Howe that a forty-foot bluff at Brewton's Hill "should be fortified and defended to the last extremity." Howe failed to heed Elbert's advice and placed only forty men on the bluff.[26]

Lieutenant Colonel Archibald Campbell—the commander of the British expedition—sent scouts on two flatboats up the river to find a landing place for his troops. "From this intelligence I proposed," Campbell wrote in his journal entry for December 26, "I should push on shore in the middle of the night at Girardeau's plantation with one thousand men, and establish a footing before daylight." His plan was foiled when "the night proved so boisterous, and the wind so contrary, it was impossible to execute this service."[27]

When the weather eventually calmed, Campbell led the landing party. "On this bluff a small body of rebels appeared in readiness for our reception," Campbell reported, "having occupied the houses and barns of the plantation and knocked out planks for their firelocks to look through."

A narrow bank with deep ditches on each side crossed a soggy rice field that lay between the landing place and the bluff. The bank was so narrow that only two soldiers could march side by side as they crossed. At dawn on December 29, 1778, a corporal and four Highlanders from the 71st Regiment set out across the bank followed by a sergeant and twelve Highlanders about fifty yards back, followed by Campbell and a light infantry company of Highlanders. Altogether, five hundred British soldiers had landed. When the British approached within one hundred yards of the American position, the Americans opened fire. Campbell launched his company of light infantry in a Highland charge toward the

Americans. The Highlanders "rushed on with such rapidity that in less than three minutes we were in possession" of the bluff at Brewton's Hill, Campbell reported. "The rebels retreated with precipitation by the back doors and windows" of John Girardeau's house and barns. "This acquisition was a favorable presage of our future success and were it not for the loss of Captain Cameron, an officer of distinguished merit and bravery, who with three Highlanders were killed, and five Highlanders wounded, nothing could have turned out more fortunate."

Campbell confirmed that Howe should have heeded Elbert's advice. "Had the rebels stationed four pieces of cannon on this bluff with five hundred men for its defense," Campbell observed, "it is more than probable they would have destroyed the greatest part of this division of our little army in their progress to the bluff."

As soon as Campbell took possession of Brewton's Hill and secured the landing place, he sent out scouts who reported that the Americans had taken a defensive possession on the southern edge of the Savannah River. Wanting to attack quickly, Campbell led about two thousand soldiers into battle while the rest of his troops continued to disembark from the transports. When Campbell got within eight hundred yards of the enemy, he climbed a tall tree to study the American defenses. A marshy stream separated the British and American forces. One flank of the American army extended to marshes and rice fields beside the Savannah River. The other flank appeared to be protected by swampland.

Campbell, combining his talents as an engineer and a military tactician, looked for a way to maneuver behind the American lines. A slave from a nearby plantation told Campbell that a path led through the swamp that lay beside the right flank of the American army. Campbell sent about six hundred light infantrymen across the path through the swamp while the main body of his command prepared to assault the center of the American position.[28]

The Georgia Continental brigade—what was left of it after a series of disastrous expeditions to Florida—moved into position on the left side of the American line near the Savannah River. The brigade was armed, Elbert said, with a "medley of rifles, old muskets and fowling pieces."[29]

The responsibility for defending Savannah fell on about 650 Continental troops from Georgia and South Carolina, about one hundred Georgia militiamen who were even more poorly equipped than the Continental troops, and a small artillery unit.

When the British light infantry emerged from the swamp and attacked Georgia militia at the military barracks inside Savannah, well behind the American defensive position on the edge of town, General Howe ordered the American defenders to retreat. The South Carolina brigade withdrew first, the artillery unit went next, and Elbert brought the Georgia brigade into position to cover the rear of the retreat. General Howe reported that Elbert's brigade withdrew from the battle line in "perfect good order."

The South Carolina brigade moved quickly enough to escape from town before the British light infantry cut off the line of retreat. Elbert's Georgia brigade fell behind and came under fire from the British light infantry. Another British detachment cut off the line of retreat along the Augusta Road leading out of Savannah to the west. Elbert decided to fight through what he considered a weak stretch of the British line so that his brigade could escape down the Ogeechee Road to the south. Elbert issued orders: "Halt! Sections, to the left face: By files to the right wheel: March." The brigade broke ranks, however, and most of the Georgians fled down the road into Savannah.

Elbert went with his men and continued to look for an escape route. Another officer told Elbert that a makeshift bridge of logs had been built across Musgrove Creek at Yamacraw on the far edge of Savannah. Elbert waved his sword above his head and shouted, "Follow me, soldiers, and I will conduct you to a safe retreat." When the soldiers reached the bank of Musgrove Creek, however, they could not find a bridge. The creek was at high tide, and if there ever was a bridge then it must have been underwater. They had no choice, Elbert told his men, other than to swim across the tide-swollen creek. Most of the men decided not to take the risk. Elbert and a few officers and men did manage to swim to the far shore and escape. The 186 remaining soldiers were trapped at the bank of the creek. When British attackers opened fire on the Americans, a Georgia major who had stayed behind because he could not swim raised a white flag and surrendered to a British lieutenant.[30]

Campbell wrote in his journal, "it was flood tide, and such only who could swim effected their escape. Among these, General Robert Howe, Colonels Huger and Elbert were successful, but they left their horses in the mud."[31] Campbell's well-conceived attack killed eighty-three American defenders, wounded eleven, and took 488 prisoners, while the British lost only seven killed and nineteen wounded. In a single day, Campbell had driven the American forces out of Georgia, seized the American artillery, small arms, shot, gunpowder and other military stores, and occupied Georgia's capital. Campbell bragged that he was the first British officer to tear a stripe and star out of the Continental flag.[32]

On the day after the battle, Howe reported:

> I am much indebted to Colonel Huger of the 5th South Carolina Regiment and to Colonel Elbert of the 2nd of

Georgia for their conduct through the whole day—Colonel Huger headed a party and made a stand at a defile through which we were obliged to retreat, and by checking the enemy rendered us signal service—and Colonel Elbert for the order in which he kept his men, and the officer-like direction of his light infantry has high merit. The well-conducted fire of that corps does honor to Major Moore who commanded it.

Colonel Roberts of the corps of artillery deserves great praise for every part of his conduct but particularly that through a sandy road with tired horses he managed so well to bring off three field pieces out of four through a hot, long-continued fire—nor would he have lost one piece had not the driver of it been killed.

Colonel Walton of the militia behaved in a manner which did him great honor; sorry I am to add that by a wound in the thigh he fell into the enemy's hands. The militia under his command, who formed part of our right, behaved exceedingly well, particularly the company of artillery under the command of Major Woodruff, who notwithstanding a hot fire maintained against great odds for some time a field piece which seemed to be well directed and for which the major deserves great commendation.

Colonel McIntosh and Colonel Harris were active and spirited. In short, both officers and men behaved well, and considering that they were troops few of which had seen action, their number not exceeding 600, retreating for a long way under the fire of a well-disciplined enemy (greatly superior in numbers) no more could be expected from them that what they performed.[33]

AFTER CAMPBELL CAPTURED SAVANNAH, British General Augustine Prevost left East Florida and marched up the Georgia coast, capturing the fortified port of Sunbury. As Prevost approached Savannah, Campbell moved out of the best house in town to let Prevost move in. General Prevost arrived at Savannah in mid-January of 1779 and immediately took command of the army that Campbell had brought to Georgia.[34]

Campbell told a friend that Prevost, at age fifty-nine, "seems a worthy man, but too old and inactive for this service. He will do in garrison, and I shall gallop with the light troop."[35] While Prevost commanded the garrison in Savannah, Campbell intended to gallop with the light troop to Augusta. Campbell set out in late January of 1779 with about a thousand British and loyalist troops. He planned to link up with additional loyalist units coming from the backcountry and also planned to recruit civilians to form loyalist militia.

On January 25, Campbell sent the light infantry to secure a bridge across Brier Creek. "These troops surprised a body of the enemy," Campbell wrote, "and were in sufficient time to save the bridge, which was actually in flames. Some prisoners fell into our hands on this occasion." Brier Creek, Campbell reported, "is about one hundred feet wide at the bridge, and about eight or ten feet in depth; the current of water is slow, and the bottom muddy." Campbell enrolled several men from the Brier Creek neighborhood into the militia and directed them to "keep within the circle of their respective farms, and to fix upon a place of rendezvous in case of an alarm." He established a post at Brier Creek manned with thirty Carolina loyalists and twenty rifle dragoons. He fortified the post with an abbatis—a defensive structure made of tree trunks and limbs—around houses.

Under Prevost's orders, Campbell reluctantly sent the Florida Rangers under Thomas Brown to attack patriots in Burke County. The patriots defeated the Rangers and wounded Brown.[36]

GEORGIA'S CONTINENTAL OFFICERS—including John McIntosh and Samuel Elbert—were forced to flee from Georgia during the British capture of Savannah but they did not abandon Georgia. Under orders from Southern Department commander Benjamin Lincoln, Elbert traveled up the South Carolina side of the Savannah River with plans take command of 150 Continental troops stationed in Augusta.[37] By the end of January, Elbert was in the backcountry of Georgia, joining forces with several other patriot officers.[38]

Campbell reported that Elbert was at Telfair's sawmill, about twenty-four miles away from Campbell's army, on January 28. Campbell set out at four o'clock in the morning to confront Elbert but, by the time Campbell reached Telfair's sawmill, Elbert was no longer there. Campbell sent a spy to "examine General Elbert's situation." As night approached, fifty patriot horsemen pursued the spy close to the lines of Campbell's camp. "By the agility of the spy's horse, he escaped," Campbell reported, "and our dragoons in turn pursued and took two of the rebels, from whom I received confirmation of Colonel Brown's intelligence respecting the junction of General Elbert, Colonels Hammond, Ingram and Few; and that the enemy had taken post at Boggy Gut to dispute our progress."[39]

Campbell hoped to attack Elbert's force. When the British reached Boggy Gut shortly after daybreak on January 29, however, they found nothing but traces of the Americans' campfires. By noon, spies and scouts informed Campbell that Elbert intended to oppose the British advance at a deep, swampy ravine called Macbean's

Creek. At two hours before midnight, the British light infantry and Florida Rangers started secretly working their way through the dark woods to a bluff overlooking Elbert's camp. At two hours after midnight, the main body of Campbell's troops started advancing toward Elbert's position. At four o'clock in the morning of January 30, Campbell arranged his troops for battle.

At daylight British artillery pounded Elbert's position. Seeing no response, Campbell sent his infantry across the creek. They found pots of beef and pork on fires lighted so recently that the water in the pots was just slightly warm. They also found blankets, muskets and provisions that had been left behind by the Americans. All the evidence showed that Elbert had abandoned his position in a hurry. Elbert had captured two Florida Rangers searching for plunder who told him of Campbell's plan for a surprise attack. Elbert managed to withdraw from Macbean's Creek just half an hour before artillery fire signaled the start of the attack.[40]

Elbert fell back ten miles along the road to Augusta. At Spirit Creek, his force of two hundred men took shelter in a small stockade called Fort Henderson. On January 30 Campbell placed a howitzer and two six-pounder cannons on a piece of high ground three hundred yards from the stockade. British artillery fire smashed into the stockade and struck several American soldiers. The Americans scrambled out the stockade "in a very precipitate manner," Campbell reported, but remained in battle formation near Spirit Creek. Campbell's army crossed the creek, occupied the stockade, and formed for battle with the right flank against the stockade. Elbert led the Americans in a retreat toward Augusta.[41]

Campbell received intelligence that Elbert's command had been reinforced and lay in ambush at a swamp called the Cupboard. When the British cautiously approached the Cupboard on January

31 they found no resistance, indicating that the intelligence was false or that the Americans had withdrawn.[42]

After reaching Augusta, Elbert crossed the Savannah River and joined forces with Andrew Williamson, a South Carolina brigadier general. American records indicated a combined forced of twelve hundred men, but Campbell thought he faced eighteen hundred men.[43]

CAMPBELL'S ARMY continued toward Augusta and entered the town early in the evening of January 31, 1779, without resistance. Campbell occupied Augusta for two weeks. He deployed his troops in defensive positions and strengthened the town's fortifications. During the occupation an event occurred that would soon have drastic repercussions. A marauding band of patriots killed Sergeant Hugh MacAlister of the 71st Regiment while he protected a patriot family from reprisals by local loyalists. Campbell described the event in his journal entry for February 3:

> The enemy appeared to have no disposition to disturb us, otherways than by sending a number of small parties across the Savannah River to plunder the inhabitants... One of these parties shot and cruelly cut with hatchets one of our most valuable light infantry men (named MacAlister) who had been placed as a safeguard at the house of a rebel major, about one mile from camp. This major was a prisoner of war in my possession, and entreated in pressing terms to grant him a safeguard for the protection of his wife and family.
>
> The barbarity which accompanied this murder was disgraceful in the extreme and I was in hopes that the rebels would have afforded me instant and ample redress, as

General Williamson disclaimed the act and, it is said, loaded the perpetrators with irons; but instead of punishing them with promptness according to their deserts, he sent them to General Lincoln at Purrysburg, who directed their irons to be struck off, and there the business ended. The British troops, however, were greatly exasperated by this shameful act of injustice; especially the light infantry who had determined to avenge MacAlister's murder on the first favorable occasion.[44]

On February 11 Campbell learned that patriot troops from North Carolina would arrive in the evening to reinforce Elbert and Williamson across the river from Augusta. The North Carolinians commanded by General John Ashe numbered from nine hundred to eleven hundred, according to American reports, but Campbell's spies estimated the number at sixteen hundred. Campbell believed that his army of one thousand men faced an American army of 3,800 men. Campbell recognized the risk of remaining in Augusta and on February 14 withdrew toward Savannah.

General Williamson sent three hundred mounted men to harass the British withdrawal; the makeshift cavalry contained Richmond County militia and South Carolina troops, and its officers included Lieutenant Colonel John McIntosh and Colonels Leroy Hammond and John Twiggs. Campbell followed the south side of Brier Creek to Odom's Ferry, where his troops crossed the creek on a bridge of rafts on February 17. Expecting pursuit, they installed a redoubt on the north side of Brier Creek. The American troops, however, stayed on the south side of Brier Creek as they passed the British position with the intent of burning bridges across the creek. On February 18, the American patrol led by Hammond, Twiggs and McIntosh launched a surprise attack on a British outpost at Herbert's Store on the Savannah River garrisoned by about seventy men. The Americans killed or wounded several British soldiers and forced the others to surrender. The Americans also seized two hundred horses belonging to the British army.[45]

Campbell's army found security in the fortified British post at Hudson's Ferry, forty-eight miles from Savannah.[46] Campbell, who planned to return to England after conquering Georgia, turned over command of the troops at Hudson's Ferry to Lieutenant Colonel James Mark Prevost, the younger brother of General Augustine Prevost. Campbell wrote in his journal on February 20:

> At this station I met Lieutenant Colonel Prevost, who informed me that he was in the future to command the advance troops and he should be obliged to me for my opinion and advice respecting the intentions of the rebels, which I gave with pleasure by telling him I was well persuaded, if the enemy were not disturbed, they would advance as far as Briar Creek, in which case they might be easily surprised by sending some of our troops to amuse them in front while the rest proceeded up the Back Road towards the bridge at Paris's Mills and came round upon their rear. As the colonel had never seen that country, I showed him my sketch of these parts and explained in the fullest manner the nature of the ground lying on each side of the Back Road, and that between the creek and the river.[47]

Campbell proceeded downriver to the British post at Ebenezer, where he met with General Augustine Prevost. "I took occasion to mention to the general my ideas regarding the motions of the light troops," Campbell wrote. "The probability of the rebels coming down to Briar Creek, and the facility of getting round into their rear by Paris's Mill. I showed him also my sketch of the country on both sides of Briar Creek, which seemed to give him satisfaction."[48]

When he reached Savannah, Campbell took measures to restore British colonial rule in Georgia. He issued a proclamation for enforcing the laws that governed Georgia in 1775 on the eve of the American Revolution. He restored the civil offices of the British colony and set up a police department for the city of Savannah. At the beginning of his expedition, Campbell had been given a commission as governor of Colonial Georgia and, quite optimistically, as governor of Colonial South Carolina. The plan called for him to be replaced as governor of Georgia by the former colonial governor, James Wright, who had escaped from Savannah when the revolution began. On March 4 Campbell appointed a lieutenant governor pro tempore to serve as the chief civil executive from the time Campbell left Georgia until the time Wright arrived. He chose James Mark Prevost because "being the brother of General Prevost, who was so much attached to his welfare and success that there is not a doubt but harmony and unanimity will take place between the civil and military branches of the government."[49]

HOPING TO CATCH the British troops on their return march from Augusta, the Americans commanded by General Ashe marched down the Georgia side of the Savannah River. When they arrived at Brier Creek on February 27, they set up camp at the foot of Miller Bridge. While Ashe attended a council of war at Purrysburg, Colonel Elbert of Georgia persuaded the general commanding the North Carolina brigade to move the camp onto higher ground a mile upstream from Miller Bridge. A light infantry detachment of about two hundred men fit for duty commanded by Lieutenant Colonel Anthony Lytle remained at Miller Bridge.

The main encampment occupied a large farm field near a fork in Brier Creek, providing the troops with a convenient source of water. A vast swamp stretched nearly three miles to the Savannah River on the side of the encampment opposite from Brier Creek. The road to Miller Bridge intersected with the road to Augusta at the camp.[50]

The soldiers in camp could not build defensive works because they did not have entrenching tools. They were not issued ammunition because they did not have cartridge boxes. Supplies were nearly impossible to get because Ashe had posted their supply train eight miles away at Burton's Ferry.

The American army remained at Brier Creek for four days waiting for reinforcements. Ashe complained that only 207 mounted soldiers from South Carolina joined him, and only 150 of them were fit for duty. The force available to Ashe contained General John Bryant's brigade of nine hundred North Carolinians, about a hundred Georgia Continentals—including John McIntosh—as well as Georgia militia. A four-pound field piece and a pair of two-pound swivels mounted as field pieces constituted the American artillery at Brier Creek.

On the other side of the Savannah River, Major John Grimke's South Carolina artillery and Brigadier General Griffith Rutherford's North Carolina regiment of seven hundred infantry arrived at Matthews Bluff. The American plan called for them to cross the river and march three miles to the camp at Brier Creek. Fifty men began building bridges and clearing a road across the swamp from the Georgia side of the Savannah River to the camp at Brier Creek, but they did not complete the job. "The river was very full by reason of the late rains," remembered American soldier James Fergus, "the backwater extended up the creek twelve miles at least to where it was fordable from where we lay."[51]

Major Francis Ross led sixty American horsemen to gather intelligence on March 1. A local woman informed them that British troops encamped nearby would soon drive the Americans out of the area. The horsemen returned to camp on March 2. Ashe returned from Purrysburg a few hours after Ross returned from Paris's Mill, but did not consult with Ross until later in the day. Either Ross did not tell Ashe that British troops were on the way or Ashe did not believe the intelligence to be accurate. Ross apparently told Ashe that his men were exhausted from their long march and overnight scouting expedition, so Ashe did not order them to scout on the night of March 2. The Americans, therefore, did not discover that a British force was bearing down on them.[52]

Nearly four hundred British soldiers of the 1st Battalion of the 71st Regiment took a position across Brier Creek from the Americans on March 2. While the Americans watched that battalion, Colonel James Mark Prevost led a force of nine hundred British soldiers on a fifty-mile march to come around behind the Americans. The British force on the march included the 2nd Battalion of the 71st Regiment under the command of Colonel John Maitland. About forty men of the 71st formed a dragoon company using cavalry equipment seized in Savannah. Sir James Baird commanded two companies of light infantry. The force also included three companies of elite troops of the 60th Regiment, and fifty men of the Florida Rangers. The British crossed Brier Creek at Paris's Mill, upstream of the American army. The maneuver trapped the

Americans between Brier Creek, the Savannah River and the British force.

On the morning of March 3, Ashe sent Ross with about 160 horsemen to scout the area between Brier Creek and Hudson's Ferry. While Ross was on patrol, he found evidence that British troops were on the move towards Paris's Mill, but he did not relay the information to the American camp at Brier Creek.[53]

Colonel Leonard Marbury, a veteran of the American campaigns along the Georgia-Florida frontier, led a band of dragoons on a reconnaissance mission toward Paris's Mill. The dragoons encountered British troops and exchanged shots. Marbury attempted to send a messenger to warn the Americans at the camp on Brier Creek, but the British captured the messenger. Another American horseman, however, also saw the British force and raced back to the camp. Shortly after he arrived, a messenger came from the detachment guarding the baggage train at Burton's Ferry eight miles from the encampment and reported that a large British force was approaching the American position.[54]

Colonel Elbert of Georgia and General Bryant of North Carolina joined commanding officer General Ashe for a quick conference. They agreed that the Americans would have to stand and fight. The Americans distributed ammunition under imminent threat of attack. Some of the soldiers received ammunition that did not match the caliber of their weapons. Because the soldiers did not have cartridge boxes, they stuffed ammunition into their shirts or cradled cartridges in their elbows.

The British force reached the American camp at 3 p.m. on March 3, 1779, and drove back the pickets. As the Americans scrambled to take defensive positions, the British infantry advanced at the quick step and the British artillery opened fire.[55] Ashe told Elbert "Sir, you had better advance and engage them."[56]

About nine hundred British soldiers attacked the American camp. Captain Baird's light infantry faced the American left flank along the Brier Creek swamp. The 2nd Battalion of the 71st occupied the center. North Carolina provincials and Florida Rangers faced the American right flank. Fifty loyalist riflemen took position to shoot down patriots attempting to flee toward the Savannah River. The grenadiers of the 60th Regiment and dragoons led by Thomas Trawse hovered in reserve. Prevost placed his five artillery pieces in the center, to the rear of the 2nd Battalion of the 71st Highlanders.[57]

American rosters listed about eleven hundred troops at Brier Creek, but detachments had reduced the number significantly; there may have been as few as six hundred troops in the main encampment. Georgia Continentals and militia, totaling about a hundred men, occupied the center of the American line. North Carolina militia from New Bern formed on the left beside Brier Creek, while North Carolina militia from Edenton took position on the right toward the Savannah River swamp. North Carolina militia from Halifax and Wilmington formed the second line.

The entire battle lasted only about fifteen minutes, and most of the Americans fled within five minutes after the initial attack. The Georgians fired two volleys, and the British returned fire. Then, according to Ashe, the Georgians "advanced without orders a few steps beyond the line and moved to the left in front of the regiment from the district of New Bern, which much impeded their firing." The militia from Edenton moved slightly to the right. The combined movements of the Georgians to the left and the North Carolinians to the right created a gap in the American line.[58]

The troops in the center of the British line launched a bayonet charge into the gap. Many of the American militiamen ran away without firing a shot. The Wilmington men and some of the New Bern men fired a few volleys and stood their ground waiting for reinforcements. The militia unit from Edenton fled from the British bayonets, and the rest of the North Carolina militia panicked and joined the flight.

"The line was just formed as we arrived to the left wing commanded by Colonel Elbert," said James Fergus, a member of a mounted regiment from South Carolina. "We rode close along the rear of the line when the first general fire was made; as we were on lower ground than the enemy, it passed chiefly over our heads. We had got to the extremity of the right wing where General Ashe commanded by the time the second fire was made. This was our post, but we had not time to give more than one fire when the general wheeled and fled and the whole wing with him. He was gone about 150 yards or more before our little party followed."[59]

Lytle's detachment rushed from its position at Miller Bridge and came within a hundred yards of the British line; two of Lytle's men were wounded. Lytle's men moved against a tide of Americans fleeing into the swamps. Lytle tried to march his men from the battlefield in good military order.[60]

The battle gave the Highlanders in the British force an occasion to avenge the death of Hugh MacAlister, the sergeant whose body had been hacked with hatchets in Augusta. Second-hand accounts of the battle reported to Archibald Campbell in Savannah said that "...when the light infantry were running up in line to charge the rebels, one of the Highlanders called out – *Now my Boys, remember poor Macalister:* in consequence of which, this corps spared very few that came within their reach."[61]

Colonel Elbert and Lieutenant Colonel McIntosh motivated a band of Continental troops and Georgia militia to stand and fight. The Georgians realized that the American right wing had evaporated when they discovered British soldiers attacking from behind their position.[62] The band kept fighting until the British killed, wounded, or captured each Georgian. Both McIntosh and Elbert were wounded before they surrendered.[63]

While the British concentrated on subduing the Georgians, the other American soldiers grasped an opportunity to escape. One soldier fled so quickly that he left his boots in camp. The fugitives sloshed through three miles of swamp to reach the Savannah River. "General Ashe rode a good horse, left his men, and got round the enemy and made to a ferry above, crossed, and escaped," Fergus said, "while the rest of us were drove into the swamp between the creek and the river. The banks of these were so steep and deep that the horses that went in could not get out again, and some men would have been drowned had not canes been put into their hands and helped them out. We now got into a thick canebreak, and the enemy pursued us no farther. This was late in the evening." [64]

When they reached the Savannah River, the fugitives discarded hundreds of hats, shirts, canteens and firearms. Forced to choose between clothes and a rifle, many soldiers chose to keep their rifles as they prepared to plunge into the cold, swift, deep water.[65]

Rather than attempting to swim across the river, some Americans found a way to float across. "Twelve of us got together," Fergus said, "and, as it was moonlight in the night, we formed a small raft of driftwood in the mouth of a lagoon, on which three of us with danger and much difficulty got over the river, after being carried above a mile down before we landed."

On the South Carolina side of the river, Fergus said, "We got out of the bottom and wandered up the river till daylight." Fergus and his comrades found a rowboat loaded with ears of corn. "Opposite to us on the other bank we discovered a great number of the North Carolina men," Fergus said. Risking their safety for the sake of soldiers stranded on the Georgia side, Fergus and his comrades "quickly rowed over and took in as many as the boat would bear and caused them to throw out the corn while we crossed back. By this means we got all our men that were there off before the enemy came down to the river." [66]

"Poor fellows!" exclaimed General William Moultrie, who was stationed downriver at Purrysburg at the time of the battle. "Most of them threw down their arms," Moultrie said, "and ran through a deep swamp, two or three miles, to gain the banks of a wide and rapid river, and plunged themselves in, to escape from the bayonet; many of them endeavoring to reach the opposite shore, sunk down, and were buried in a watery grave; while those who had more strength, and skill in swimming, gained the other side, but were still so terrified, that they straggled through the woods in every direction."[67]

The Americans who crossed the river continued to suffer. Fergus observed, "Many of our men were half-naked, having stripped to swim the river. The third of March we were defeated, and that night there was a light frost, and many suffered in the cold, having nothing on but a shirt or breeches. Here we lay, I know not how long."[68]

As the survivors of the Battle of Brier Creek emerged from the swamps on the South Carolina side of the Savannah River, they behaved more like refugees than soldiers. Most of the survivors walked to their homes in North Carolina without stopping anywhere along the way. They had a chance to go home because their comrades from Georgia fought while they fled. [69]

The British scored a decisive victory at the Battle of Brier Creek. Their casualties were relatively light: one British officer and five privates died in the battle, and ten British soldiers suffered wounds. The British captured the American artillery, about a thousand muskets and all of the American supplies, provisions and equipment.

Throughout the war, commanders often exaggerated their successes, and that may have been the case when Augustine Prevost boasted that "Brigadier General Elbert, one of their best officers, several more of note, in the whole twenty-seven officers, were taken, with near two hundred men." Prevost reported "about 150 killed on the field of battle and adjoining woods and swamps; but their chief loss consists in the number of officers and men drowned in attempting to save themselves from the slaughter, and plunging into a deep and rapid river."[70]

The British victory at Brier Creek carried significant consequences. British officials continued to implement colonial rule in Georgia, and Governor James Wright returned to Savannah on July 14, 1779, four months after the battle. The British military maintained control of Savannah and coastal Georgia until the war was practically finished. From their base in Savannah, the British moved northward, captured Charleston, and set up a chain of posts across the South Carolina backcountry. The British occupied Augusta from May of 1780 until June of 1781, temporarily exerting control over all of Georgia. Those gains would have been stopped or at least delayed if the American campaign to wrest Georgia from British control had not ended in disaster at Brier Creek.

American General William Moultrie recognized the significance of the Battle of Brier Creek in the progress of the American Revolution. "This unlucky affair at Brier Creek disconcerted all our plans," Moultrie said, "and through the misfortunes of General Howe and General Ashe the war was protracted at least one year longer."[71]

MCINTOSH REMAINED a prisoner of war for more than a year following the Battle of Brier Creek.[72] After he was exchanged, he volunteered to serve with the Georgia militia through the campaign of 1781 and for a time was an aide to the South Carolina partisan leader General Thomas Sumter.[73] Legendary deeds were attributed to the dashing young officer. For instance, the story goes, in 1781 he fought a duel with Lieutenant Augustus George Christian Elholm.[74] Here is a romantic account of that deed:

> ...McIntosh, when a Lieutenant Colonel in the army of the Revolution, during the war became acquainted with Miss Sarah Swinton, of South Carolina, of Scottish descent, and whose father, a patriot of those times, was killed in battle by the British at Stono. Her form was light and delicate. Possessed of a well-cultivated and discriminating mind, with a rare faculty for conversation and argument, and although of retiring manners, she espoused with an almost imprudent zeal the cause of freedom, in a part of the country infested by Tories, and marauding bands of British troops. To this lady he was engaged to be married; and in one of his excursions to the neighbourhood in which she resided, he was informed that Captain Elholm, a Polander in the American service (Lee's Legion), had acted oppressively

towards some of the inhabitants, and on remonstrating with him on the injustice and impolicy of his conduct, a quarrel quickly ensued, and which, it was promptly determined, should be settled by the arbitrament of the sword.

... Both were young, resolute, active, and powerful men, and it was thought that one or both would certainly be killed in the contest; and as the parties were moving to the place of combat, Miss Swinton requested to see for an instant her intended consort... He called on her, and was met with serious distress, and after a little conversation, she observed, "If you are, then, inviolably pledged to meet this man, and feel that your honour is dearer than life, what shall I do?" [She soon] fled to her room, to conceal there her agitation and the anguish of a devoted heart.

The hostile parties met under a large oak... At the word "Ready," they drew, and, advancing with sharp and glittering swords, commenced the battle in good earnest, with firm hearts and sturdy arms. In a little time the right arm of Captain Elholm was nearly severed from his body, and fell powerless by his side. ...His sword was dexterously transferred to his left hand, which he used with great effect; and the blows came so awkwardly, that they were not easily parried by his right-handed antagonist. Both were in a few moments disabled in such a manner, that the friends present felt it proper to interfere, and end the bloody conflict.

They carried to their graves the scars, and deeply furrowed cheeks, as evidences of a once terrible struggle. Miss Swinton was not long in suspense; the combatants were soon taken from the field, disfigured by many deep and dangerous sabre wounds, of which, in due time, they both recovered; and the Colonel often remarked that he was more indebted to the tender attentions of Miss S. for his restoration to health than to the management or skill of his surgeon...

A little time after this occurrence, Colonel McIntosh brought his young and patriotic wife to Georgia, his native State."[75]

John McIntosh and his relatives, among the most prominent and prosperous families in Georgia before the American Revolution, struggled to recover from the ravages of war. While the men had been off at war, their plantations had been plundered and damaged by American troops, loyalist raiders, and British occupiers. "This cursed war has ruined us all," John's uncle Robert Baillie observed to another uncle, General Lachlan McIntosh.[76]

Baillie described the financial situation of John's father William as "really much distressed." Baillie added, "My own situation is indeed very little better for though I am not yet sued, the debts I owe, with interest accumulating for these five years past, amounts to a sum I shall never be able to pay and my property is so greatly reduced that I can hardly support my family in any decent manner."[77]

John himself "lost the greatest part of his private fortune" in the war, said his uncle Lachlan, and later "was unguardedly taken in by speculators, which involved him in debt."[78]

When Spanish authorities loosened rules for immigrating into East Florida in 1790, John McIntosh saw an opportunity to escape his financial woes. East Florida—which had been ceded to Spain by England at the end of the American Revolution—needed residents to provide economic development and military security. English-speaking Protestants could receive land grants if they would become citizens of East Florida and swear allegiance to the Spanish government. John decided to "remove to the Province of East Florida," his uncle Lachlan said, "to do justice to his creditors without immediate injury to his family."[79]

Rebel in East Florida

JOHN MCINTOSH DEFIED financial difficulties in Georgia by moving to Spanish East Florida. John brought his wife Sarah and their six children to a plantation on the south side of the St. Johns River by 1791. The plantation was known as Cerro Fuente, meaning Spring Hill, but Sarah referred to it as Bellevue. John also owned other property, including a plantation on the north side of the St. Johns at Cowford on the site that later became Jacksonville.[1] John authorized his brother William to sell John's land in Georgia and to receive cattle in payment; John intended to bring the cattle to his new plantations in East Florida.[2]

Although Spanish officials commissioned John McIntosh as a magistrate and gave him authority as lieutenant governor of East Florida in the St. Johns district,[3] tension arose between the Spanish authorities and Anglo settlers like the McIntosh family. Irritants included Spanish policies on slavery, trade, travel, and Indian relations.[4]

SLAVERY ISSUES created tension for centuries between Spanish officials in East Florida and residents of South Carolina and Georgia. Spain ruled Florida during the Colonial period until 1763, and Great Britain ruled Georgia, South Carolina and the other North American colonies along the Atlantic coast. In the British colonies, slaves were seldom freed and free black communities rarely developed. Under Spanish law, slaves could purchase their freedom or have someone else purchase it on their behalf, and masters could grant freedom to slaves. A free black community developed at Mose near St. Augustine, and free black men formed a militia that participated in the defense of Florida. Because Spain offered religious sanctuary to slaves who escaped from British colonies and became baptized Catholics, runaway slaves poured into Florida from Georgia and South Carolina.[5]

When Britain acquired Florida from Spain in 1763, slaves had less incentive to flee to Florida, but in the turmoil of the American Revolution slaves had more opportunities to escape from plantations in Georgia and South Carolina. When Britain ceded Florida to Spain in negotiations ending the American Revolution, slaves in Florida exploited the unstable transition process to find refuge. Incoming Spanish officials granted freedom to at least 250 persons who had been enslaved during the British occupation of Florida. The policy of granting religious sanctuary to escaped slaves resumed when Spain regained Florida, but the new United States government negotiated an end to the policy in 1790. Even then, however, runaway slaves who reached St. Augustine could petition for freedom under Spanish law; while they awaited a judicial decision, they served as slaves of the Spanish crown and provided free labor to the East Florida government.[6] John McIntosh caught a slave who had escaped from one of McIntosh's friends and kept the slave in custody while attempting to obtain permission to return the slave to Georgia; East Florida officials accused McIntosh of violating a policy requiring that slaves seeking asylum be turned over to the Spanish government.[7]

Residents of the United States attempting to recover runaway slaves were required by law to obtain permission from Spanish officials. Many slave catchers entered East Florida illegally, taking any slaves they could seize, stealing property, and committing violence against residents. As a result of such depredations, Anglo settlers like John McIntosh endured dangers of life on the frontier with little protection from the East Florida government.[8]

TRADE POLICIES depressed economic development in East Florida, especially in the northern districts where the Anglo settlers maintained relationships with businessmen in Georgia. Although the settlers lived closer to Georgia than to the Florida capital at St. Augustine, Spanish law forbade them from trading with America. John McIntosh received a passport to travel to Georgia on business, but was accused of misusing it.[9] Florida lore contains this tidbit:

> ...McIntosh was granted land by the Spanish Government and developed a plantation by the St. Johns River near the Spanish customs post of San Nicholas. There, boat loads of cotton from the south moving down the river to the sea were stopped for payment of the export duty on cotton. Whenever McIntosh had his cotton ready for export, he went to the commander at San Nicholas to await the approach of his cotton boats. As they approached in the distance the Spaniard raised his spyglass, intently inspected them, and shrugged his shoulders.
> Lowering his spyglass he turned to McIntosh: "There's too much cotton to pass without duty."
> Silently McIntosh handed him a Spanish gold doubloon.
> The commander put the doubloon to one eye, his spyglass to the other, and remarked, "I still see cotton."
> McIntosh gave him another doubloon.
> The Spaniard placed a doubloon over each eye and said contentedly, "I see no cotton now."[10]

Anglo settlers also became dissatisfied with rules on trade with the Indians. Spanish officials had given the British firm Panton, Leslie and Company permission to trade with the Indians and East Florida officials interpreted that as giving the firm a monopoly.[11] Unable to obtain official licenses to trade with the Indians, some settlers engaged in illegal trading. A settler named James Allen established a trading house on the upper St. Marys River, the border between Georgia and East Florida,. Allen traded horses and cattle with the Indians, and was accused of buying stolen livestock from the Indians and selling it to Florida residents. Allen was arrested in 1793 and turned over to John McIntosh, who was district magistrate. McIntosh apparently believed the illegal trade was in the best interest of the settlers, because he allowed Allen to continue business as usual.[12]

English businessmen also wanted to break the grip of Panton, Leslie on the Indian trade in Spanish Florida. With their backing, William Bowles opened a trading post on the Apalachicola River in January of 1792 and threatened to invade East Florida. Suspecting that Bowles would inspire Indian attacks against Florida settlers, John McIntosh made preparations to defend the St. Johns district. He volunteered to recruit fighting men, and asked the East Florida governor for guns and ammunition. Instead of acting on McIntosh's proposal, the governor sent regular Spanish army troops to protect Panton, Leslie's property. Spanish forces captured Bowles and imprisoned him in St. Augustine.

INDIAN RAIDS commenced a few months after Bowles was arrested and continued sporadically through the summer. In October, McIntosh informed the governor that John Golphin's Indian gang, described as "outlawed, wild, unruly vagabonds," threatened the settlers on the northern frontier of East Florida. Until then, McIntosh said, he had dismissed reports of danger because "I knew there were people always ready to propagate tales that might embitter the peace of their neighbours, but this news reaches me with surprisingly more truth than I expected."[13]

Golphin countered McIntosh's report by claiming to be peaceful and to want friendly terms with the Spanish; Golphin advised the governor to "pay no attention to what any person may say or tell you" that would drive a wedge between them. When the governor asked leaders of the Creek Indian nation to control Golphin, the Anglo settlers pointed out that the "robberies and disorders" did not "originate in any idea or design being entertained by the body of the Creek nation, or of any influential or orderly headmen or warriors;" in fact, the settlers said, "the mischief" was perpetrated by "an inconsiderable number of outlying vagabond Indians."[14]

McIntosh's report was proved to be accurate when Golphin's gang attacked two plantations in East Florida in April of 1793. Neighbors gathered to chase the gang, but orders from the East Florida governor prevented them from continuing the pursuit into Georgia. Telling the governor that the outlaws felt "encouraged in their career by meeting with no opposition," McIntosh urged "that some immediate step be taken for our general safety." McIntosh's fellow residents of the St. Johns district petitioned the governor for authorization "to embody, under proper officers, to raise a strong stout of good woodsmen" at government expense. The petition also requested "some soldiers to be stationed near the western settlements of St. Johns in a block house with a plentiful supply of arms and ammunition, and another at the head of Black Creek" to protect the settlers from "total ruin." The next month, McIntosh signed a document asking for a militia unit "to be embodied and armed under proper officers of their own election and to hold themselves always in readiness to assemble on short notice to repel or apprehend any vagabond of whatever description who may appear dangerous of threatening to their peace or safety."[15]

After months of prodding by the Anglo settlers, the East Florida governor approved four companies of militia to guard the northern section of the province. Despite his military experience, McIntosh did not join the militia.[16] After the militia formed in June of 1793, the spate of Indian raids subsided.[17] The militiamen, however, complained that the government imposed onerous assignments and "excessive orders." Unreliable government funding resulted in delays in payment for militia service and scarcities of supplies, equipment, clothing, and provisions for the militiamen and their horses. While the men were away from home on service, their families suffered from food shortages and other privations.[18] The lack of support for the local militia and general neglect of the northern part of East Florida caused many Anglo settlers to turn against the Spanish government of East Florida.

PERSONAL DISASTERS inflicted misery on John McIntosh in addition to the slavery issues, economic barriers and frontier violence that discouraged most of the Anglo settlers in northern East Florida. John endured "the loss of a lovely infant," his wife Sarah said, "his only daughter, on whom he doted."[19] John himself "suffered under a consumptive habit" for more than a year and his wife thought he was near death several times.[20]

A terrible accident befell Sarah "by attempting to reduce an inflammation of the breast, which fell on her eyes, and produced blindness, which the best oculists and medical men of our country, who had been employed, could not relieve."[21]

Sarah received treatment in Savannah while John remained in East Florida. An old acquaintance who visited Sarah in June of 1793 wrote to John that "she is mending fast and that she is in good spirits. She really appeared quite cheerful. The inflammation has entirely subsided and the film in one of her eyes is grown so thin that the color of the eye is easily discovered." She could not see well enough, however, to write a letter herself. In addition to the eye trouble, the visitor wrote, Sarah had an "issue on the back of the neck, which she says gives her little or no pain or inconvenience, although she has suffered considerably with them" in the past.[22]

A resident of Savannah noted that "Mrs. McIntosh was compelled to return here to advise with physicians about her eyes, being at that time almost blind." John, "anxious to see her, followed her some weeks afterward to Georgia and stayed several days."[23] According to Lachlan McIntosh, his nephew John "ventured for the first time, sick as he was, to come from East Florida to visit his wife (then under the physician's hand at Savannah) of whom he is passionately fond, and kept close in her room the whole time." The creditors who had caused John to move outside the United States allowed "very few of his most intimate friends to see him" during the time that he lingered in Savannah "on account of his disorder."[24]

THROUGH THE INFLUENCE of fellow Revolutionary War veterans, John McIntosh got caught up in a shadowy plot to overthrow the Spanish government of East Florida. Edmund Charles Genet, the French minister to the United States, instigated the plot in 1793. Because France was at war with Spain, Genet operated under instructions to support rebellion among the Spanish colonies in the Americas. Genet recruited Samuel Hammond to invade East Florida; Hammond was a Virginian who had been a prominent patriot during the American Revolution and had later moved to Georgia. Genet recruited Elijah Clark to invade West Florida; Clark was a Georgian who had distinguished himself as the "hero of the hornets' nest" during the American Revolution. Under Genet's influence, Clark gave up his position as major general in the Georgia militia to accept the rank of major general in the French service; Samuel Hammond of Augusta and his brother Abner Hammond, who lived at Temple on the Georgia side of the St. Marys River, also received French commissions.[25]

The French government recalled Genet in early 1794 at the request of President George Washington, who insisted on remaining neutral in foreign affairs. The plot Genet had hatched, however, continued to take shape even without official support. The plotters planned to invade Florida under the French flag, but to turn the territory over to the United States once the Spanish government had been defeated.[26] An officer of the French consul at Charleston said that John McIntosh and several other Anglo residents of East Florida were "not in on the secret but from their known sentiments they were counted upon for help."[27]

Rumors of the plot surfaced in Charleston and soon reached St. Augustine. In December of 1793 a resident of northern East Florida confessed to Captain Richard Lang, who commanded the Spanish dragoons in the St. Marys River district, that Samuel Hammond intended to invade East Florida with seven hundred men supported by three frigates. Lang sent the statement to Lieutenant Colonel Carlos Howard, the commander of Spanish forces in the northern part of East Florida. Lang added that "I expect to have a fuller account in a few days, which I will communicate either to you or His Excellency the Governor, as I intend to get to town on Saturday next if nothing unexpected happens."[28]

Colonel Howard soon learned details of the proposed expedition directly from one of the conspirators. On January 6, 1794, Samuel Hammond's brother Abner negotiated with Howard "about placing the provisions and war supplies of the conspiracy so that they can fall into the hands of the government, thus wrecking the proposed expedition." Abner Hammond claimed to be trying to prevent the invasion because "such a proceeding militated flagrantly against the honour and laws of the general government of the United States." Howard remained skeptical, telling the governor that "the confidence I now have in the man is more apparent than real, and it will remain so until I see all the preparations of the plotters completely under our control."[29]

John McIntosh came under suspicion partly through a business transaction with John Peter Wagnon, who had served with McIntosh in the American Revolution and had moved to St. Augustine a couple of years after McIntosh settled in East Florida. In November of 1793, McIntosh set off on a trip to Georgia to retrieve some of his cattle. Along the way, he received word that Sarah had returned to their home in East Florida after being treated in Georgia for inflammation of the eyes, so he went home to be with her. His friend Wagnon happened to be visiting the McIntosh home at the time. Wagnon asked much McIntosh would pay him to go to Georgia and bring back the cattle. McIntosh gave Wagnon a bay gelding valued at $110 and Wagnon agreed "to go into Georgia and have all such cattle as may be delivered to me by his brother William brought to this Province, the expense to be paid by him... I am not to be liable for any loss or accidents." McIntosh provided Wagnon an official East Florida passport to go to Georgia for the cattle. The passport had been issued to McIntosh personally, but he thought he could provide it to someone employed by him because the terms allowed him to be accompanied by two men. Franciso Sterling, who had stopped by the McIntosh home on the way to St. Augustine, took a message informing the governor about the arrangement between McIntosh and Wagnon.[30]

Proceeding into Georgia, Wagnon met with John's brother William in December "and informed him he was sent in by Col. John McIntosh for four hundred head of cattle." William said he would deliver the cattle "as soon as they could be collected, but at the same time advised Mr. Wagnon of the difficulty of taking them in on account of the great flood of water which then prevailed in all the rivers; on which Mr. Wagnon agreed to leave the cattle until the coming Spring."[31]

Wagnon returned from Georgia in January of 1794. When Wagnon reached the St. Marys River, the border between Georgia and East Florida, he was escorted across by an American military detachment.[32] Thomas Cryer, who owned a plantation south of the St. Marys River, reported that Wagnon "had arrived from Georgia in a boat with three Negroes with the plan of removing his wife, and quitting the province to go and live in Augusta, from whence he had just come." At lunch, Cryer "anxiously asked Wagnon what he knew" about the rumors of insurrection. Wagnon replied "that he hadn't heard a word of such an enterprise." Another man at the lunch table said "there was such business underway," and Wagnon added "Yes, yes there is something going on and you can be sure it will be carried out." After lunch, Wagnon "started on his way to the St. Johns and from there to St. Augustine seeking his wife." He promised the owner of the boat that he would return in eight days, and the owner "told him he would extend the wait with the boat one day longer than eight days."[33]

Passing through the St. Marys River district, Wagnon "spread the word among the inhabitants that a certain expedition was being planned, which was soon going to take place" and "urged them to collect their belongings immediately and flee with them to safety in Georgia, which he said he was going to do, coming for the purpose to the city to remove his wife," and said he was leaving a boat in readiness on the St. Marys River.[34] Knowing that he would not stay in East Florida, Wagnon had left his horses in Georgia at the home of William McIntosh, brother of John.[35] Wagnon reached his house in St. Augustine at dusk on January 20.[36]

As Wagnon went to get his wife out of St. Augustine, John McIntosh also went to St. Augustine. McIntosh accompanied Richard Lang, the dragoon captain who had notified Colonel Howard of the plot and promised to provide more information when he reached St. Augustine. On January 12, 1794, McIntosh and Lang stopped overnight at the home of William Jones on the St. Johns River. Jones was the father-in-law of Abner Hammond, who was visiting the Jones home at the time.[37] Hammond told Lang he believed the rumor of an invasion "was true because the Frenchmen wanted a port to land their plunder."[38]

Hammond "promised to stay two or three days at the McIntosh home" after McIntosh returned from St. Augustine. Jones subsequently showed a father-in-law's concern over Hammond's intentions, and confided, "McIntosh, I'll try to unravel this and get as much as possible out of him about the matter."[39]

As the day went on, several other men gathered at the Jones house. According to Lang, "the object of this gathering was just relaxation and social drinking, which they did all day."[40]

At one point, Jones exclaimed "he had no business with the Governor and that the Governor might kiss his ass, for he did not value him and that he could whip him in a fair fight and said that you may tell him so."[41]

The next morning McIntosh, Lang, and two other men set off on horseback toward St. Augustine.[42] As they rode along, McIntosh asked Lang, "Did you notice the words that Jones spoke?" Lang answered, "Yes." McIntosh said, "I think there must be something at the bottom of that, for I've never heard him speak so openly before." Lang said, "I think so, too."[43] Lang guessed that Jones was upset by something his son-in-law had told him, "and so he burst forth with the terms he had used."[44]

On the morning of January 14, McIntosh met with Governor Juan Nepomuceno de Quesada "trying to excuse himself with His Lordship about the trip to Georgia by John Peter Wagnon," sent by McIntosh "without any permission from the government." The governor also asked whether McIntosh had information on a proposed invasion of East Florida; McIntosh "inadequately responded to His Lordship on the details of the expedition even though given ample freedom in the questioning."[45]

After meeting with the governor, McIntosh dined at the home of John Leslie, a partner in the Indian trading firm of Panton, Leslie and Company that maintained an office in St. Augustine.[46] In the afternoon, as McIntosh and Leslie walked along the wharf, "McIntosh started a conversation in which he said he was talking to [Leslie] in confidence and friendship about the expedition planned against this province from Georgia." Leslie asked whether McIntosh had advised the governor, and McIntosh said he had not. Leslie told McIntosh "he was not doing right in keeping the news from the government (which news would be of interest to them so that they could take precautions in defense of the province). Leslie urged McIntosh to "lose no time" in reporting the news, and offered to "accompany him to the governor's house to serve to serve as an interpreter" because Leslie spoke Spanish and McIntosh did not.[47]

McIntosh and Leslie met with Quesada the next evening. Leslie "tried to excuse with His Lordship this mistake" made by McIntosh "in not telling him in the previous visit of the information on the proposed expedition." McIntosh said he had not discussed the expedition in the first meeting "because he thought it warranted discretion, and he could not use discretion with the commander of the battalion present and since people were always coming in and going out."[48] McIntosh then told Quesada that provisions had been stockpiled on the Georgia side of the St. Marys River. McIntosh had heard that nearly two thousand men had enlisted, but he had been told by Wagnon "that the enlisting of the troops is not against this province, as thought, but rather for establishing a new country or body politic in the western part of Georgia."[49]

At Clark's Inn, McIntosh conversed with Andrew Davis, a militia lieutenant from the St. Johns River district. Davis asked McIntosh "if he was sure this expedition was going to take place, which the public knew was notoriously projected against this province from the States of Georgia and South Carolina," and McIntosh "answered affirmatively, basing his opinion on the perseverance and independence of the ones planning the expedition." Davis disagreed with McIntosh, "because of the lack of means and allies to carry out the project." McIntosh and Davis continued to defend their opinions without changing the mind of either one.[50]

William Plowden also heard discussions of the expedition at Clark's Inn in the presence of McIntosh. Plowden had come to St. Augustine from his home in the St. Johns district with two Americans who asked the governor to allow them to settle in East

Florida; the governor had denied their request and had instructed Plowden to make sure they left East Florida immediately.

IN RESPONSE TO THE THREAT of invasion, Governor Quesada convened a council of war on January 16. The council ordered that McIntosh, Wagnon, Lang, and Jones be arrested. The council also authorized the arrest of William Plowden, who was, like McIntosh and Jones, an Anglo settler in the St. Johns River district. In addition, the council decided to arrest Abner Hammond, the only one of the suspects who had admitted knowing the details of the plot.

The council claimed that McIntosh, as lieutenant governor of the District of the St. Johns River, "has failed to communicate to the government as he should the schemes that are being plotted in the State of Georgia, which are public knowledge and notorious along the entire length of that [the St. Johns] river."

Further, the council complained that McIntosh had "violated government regulations by giving open protection to Diego Allen," who had continued to trade illegally with Indians in Florida even after McIntosh, as the local magistrate, had been told not to let Allen contact the Indians. The council also mentioned McIntosh's friendship with Wagnon, who was described as "perverse and under suspicion."

Finally, the council said, McIntosh "has seen and dealt with Abner Hammond, one of those planning to invade this province and in charge of collecting supplies for said expedition, and brother of the main leader of it." The council concluded that McIntosh "is suspected of conspiring with enemies of the State," The council ordered that all papers be taken from possession of the suspects, and that "somebody be sent to the house of John MacIntosh to pick up the papers he may have there so they can be scrutinized and examined."[51]

Shortly after the council meeting, an anonymous letter arrived at the governor's office accusing McIntosh, Jones and Plowden of supporting the proposed rebellion.[52]

Although the council recommended on January 16 that McIntosh "be arrested this night while he is in this city without a license from the government and without any excuse that could justify his so coming, thus increasing the suspicion against him," the governor did not order the arrest until January 20. On the evening of January 20, McIntosh, Lang, Plowden and Dr. James Hall, a Revolutionary War veteran who had settled in East Florida, visited Wagnon's house. When they asked him for news from Georgia, he mentioned "general talk" of about an "expedition, which was promoted by the French making tempting propositions to Americans who might enlist."[53]

Later in the evening, McIntosh and Lang went to Clark's Inn and joined a group of card players gambling for cigars. McIntosh and Lang left the table two or three times and went to the patio of the inn, leading one of the card players to guess "it must have been some secret matters they wanted to talk about because they would not talk about them in front of the others playing the game."[54] Lang, however, said he "got up two or three times to take a drink although he had drunk quite enough," but didn't talk "with anyone in particular."[55]

The mood of the card players turned from merriment to consternation when officials arrested McIntosh and Lang on suspicion of conspiracy against the East Florida government.[56] Wagnon's plan to move back to Georgia was thwarted when officials arrested him as well. Officials also arrested William Plowden.

Meanwhile, an escort marched to Jones' home in the St. Johns district to arrest him and his son-in-law Abner Hammond. Jones described having "his arms secured fast behind his back with a rope, & compelled to get on a very lame, tired horse, by which his frequent stumbling caused a hurt in one of his arms, which has terminated in the loss of the use of it, & in that situation conveyed to St. Augustine."[57]

McIntosh and the other suspects were confined to cells inside the Castillo de San Marcos. Jones complained of being "close confined in the calabooce, the floor of which was always wet & whenever it rained covered in water, in that cold season not allowed fire to keep him warm, deprived of the benefit of the light & all sort of communication, scarcely allowed enough air to keep life."[58]

Investigators searched the suspects' homes and seized papers that cast further suspicion on McIntosh. Among the papers were four letters from Samuel Hammond, the alleged commander of the expedition. Samuel Hammond, like McIntosh, had served as a lieutenant colonel in the American Revolution. The two patriots became friends and kept in touch after McIntosh moved to East Florida.[59] Their correspondence "contained "nothing more than might naturally be expected from an old acquaintance and brother officer," Sarah McIntosh insisted, confident that "Colonel Hammond's letters will speak for themselves."[60] A letter written in June of 1793, however, referred to "trouble with the Indians," which Spanish officials construed to be a code phrase for the expedition to East Florida:

> We are still in trouble with the Indians. A detachment marched from Savannah yesterday for the frontier, and another goes today, and I shall follow tomorrow. Politics are

strangely charged here [in Georgia]. I, who never sought the dame of popularity and who six months ago could scarcely make interest enough to keep out of long ships, am now as popular as any of the dons of this place. The troops will not march without me; and I have been overpersuaded to take command again.[61]

On January 21, the day after McIntosh was arrested, the government took action to defend East Florida against invaders. A council of war decided to move the line of defense from the border with Georgia on the St. Marys River farther south to the St. Johns River. The council ordered Lieutenant Colonel Howard to remove artillery and military supplies from the northern edge of the province and to burn "everything else under his command that could be of use to the enemy." To further hinder an enemy advance, the council told Howard to "advise the residents of the St. Marys and Nassau rivers to the north of the St. Johns River that anyone who wants to stay in the province and take up arms in its defense should within eight days retire to the southern side of [the St. Johns] with all his property, including boats and canoes, which it is indispensable that they keep on the [south bank of the St. Johns], within a week, burning behind them all their houses and ranches."[62] This order dismayed all the settlers in the affected area and alienated even the residents who had been loyal to the government until that point. Instead of moving southward, many of the settlers abandoned their property and sought safety in Georgia.[63]

BROUGHT FOR QUESTIONING before Governor Quesada on January 23, McIntosh "was put under oath before God Almighty and the Holy Bible of the Protestant faith which he professes, by which he swore to tell the truth of what he knew and was asked." The governor first asked what McIntosh knew of the expedition against East Florida; McIntosh replied that he didn't know any more "than that which he had already told His Lordship on the night of the fifteenth of this month, that is to say, that he had heard vaguely of the expedition."[64]

The interrogation next probed the relationship between McIntosh and the Hammond brothers. McIntosh claimed not to know the first name of the son-in-law of William Jones and said "he was not a friend of Hammond, whom he hardly knows by sight." McIntosh had said, he admitted, that "he would be glad" if Hammond "would visit him for two or three days" when McIntosh returned from St. Augustine, but Hammond had replied "that he did not know if he would have any free time."[65]

McIntosh told the questioners that "he does know and has spoken to" Samuel Hammond. Following up on their suspicion over the "Indian troubles" letter from Hammond to McIntosh, the questioners wanted to know whether "Samuel Hammond with whom he keeps in touch has written to him lately or at some other time concerning anything related to the planned invasion, and if so, what and when." McIntosh said "Samuel Hammond has never written him a word related to said invasion."[66]

The interrogation turned to Wagnon's trip to Georgia using McIntosh's passport, implying not only that Wagnon's journey was related to the invasion but also that McIntosh's cattle would be used to provision the invaders. Accused of sending Wagnon "without any permission from the government," McIntosh claimed to be "authorized by the passport," which allowed McIntosh to be accompanied on his travels by three or four other men.[67] Going back in time to when McIntosh first applied for a permit to bring in the cattle, the governor recalled that McIntosh had been "denied this on the terms he wanted (that is to be able to send the person he would choose); being told by His Lordship that it had to be a personal pass." McIntosh had said at the time "he did not know whom he was going to send." The governor had offered to wait until McIntosh chose someone for the task and applied for "a personal permit." McIntosh had then said he himself would go "personally." Based on that conversation, the interrogators concluded, McIntosh should have "come to the conclusion that one had to give the names of people in the permits to avoid such fraud as the one Wagnon wanted to work."[68]

The line of questioning shifted to the escapades of Diego Allen, who had carried on an illegal trade with the Indians in the East Florida area.

> Asked if he knew Diego Allen had enlisted in this expedition against the province after he escaped from here, protected by the witness [McIntosh] and William Jones and John Peter Wagnon:
>
> He said he does not know if Allen enlisted, and that it is not true that he [Allen] had escaped from the province under the witness's protection, because he was away at the time.
>
> Asked if the government (having had to make the determination to deprive Allen of all contact with the Indians because it was harmful) did not place him under the care of the witness as a Judge on the St. Johns River, making him stay near the witness and telling the witness, among other things, under no circumstances to let him join the Indians; and did not the witness, notwithstanding this, allow or overlook his going to them on two occasions; so His Lordship,

being suspicious of the witness, commissioned Andrew Atkinson to arrest Allen; and that the witness, having verified this, pressed for his immediate release, and not having accomplished his purpose, asked to be permitted to take him before His Lordship, who freed him on the ardent petition of the witness and Thomas Sterling; not punishing the disobediences and misdeeds of Allen, but complying with their requests, being confident of their promises that they would answer for Allen's conduct to allow him to establish himself at Matanzas from then on; but was not the result of all this, during the voluntary absence of the witness to Georgia and the illness of Sterling, that Allen escaped in the meantime, assisted by William Jones who bought his things and by John Peter Wagnon who also helped:

He said it was true what is being said about when Allen was to be established and true about the witness being in charge of not letting him visit the Indians, and that he nevertheless went two times; but the first time he was authorized by His Lordship so that he could go get the things he had left there and when the second visit was made the witness was very ill and unconscious.

That it is not true that he pressed Andrew Atkinson to free Allen, but it is true that he asked him to turn him over to His Lordship as was verified, pleading for him along with Thomas Sterling, who wanted to answer for Allen on the matter of his second visit to the Indians, blaming himself for it; and that he does not remember Sterling ever talking to him about the last recommendations of His Lordship about Allen's conduct after he told him to go live in Matanzas, because he would never obligate himself to answer for his conduct or the fulfillment of that command.⁶⁹

At the end of the hearing, a translator showed McIntosh an English-language transcript. McIntosh agreed that everything "in the statement is in accordance with what he has said: and it is affirmed and ratified; and that he is thirty-eight years old and signed with His Lordship and with the Counsellor and the Interpreter, on oath."⁷⁰

DURING LANG'S INTERROGATION, officials sought evidence that he and McIntosh had conspired to weaken the defenses on the border between Georgia and East Florida. Lang was interrogated at length about his recommendation, as captain of the local militia, to abandon a fort on the St. Marys River.

> Asked the reason for his insistence to His Lordship, by spoken and written word, that the stockade and fortified house of San Jose be abandoned, because the governor had assured him that, although there was no reason to suspect the Indians, there being complete harmony with them and no belief such a house should be built just for fear of them, but nevertheless it was needed to defend against bad people, whether Indian or white, who were around about, trying to steal, the defendant [Lang] always insisting on his opinion; but His Lordship trying to persuade him of the usefulness of such a house, mainly because if the invasion took place such a position would be where the enemy would come by on their passage into the province, and the defendant insisting on his

opinion against such a reasonable judgment, saying that four pickets were but little defense:

He said that establishing such a house as living quarters for the Commander of the River Lieutenant Colonel Carlos Howard, with a capable military detachment and store for the Indians, was always approved by the defendant because that way there was no basis for his suspicion that the Indians would be dangerous; but that the commander having retired to another post and leaving this one undermanned at a distance of ten miles from the houses of the residents, the defendant thinks that such a fortified house could do no good; rather, on the contrary, the enemy could easily take it in case of invasion and fortify themselves in it and that this could be dangerous; also that the house, because of its location, is exposed to being set afire.[71]

The officials were suspicious of McIntosh because he had talked Lang out of resigning as a captain in the East Florida militia, implying that McIntosh wanted the militia to be controlled by an ally in the event of an invasion from Georgia.

Asked if it were true that not long ago in a conversation with McIntosh he had said he wanted to leave the militia.

He said that not only did he tell McIntosh this, but he also told Lieutenant Colonel Carlos Howard the same thing, telling them that such a commission was too burdensome and took up too much time, time that he should be spending in work to maintain his family; that there was not a month that went by when this duty failed to occupy him five or six days; that since there was no salary this was unbearable; and also that he could never please the lieutenant colonel; and that McIntosh advised him not to leave the company, suggesting that Andrew Atkinson was also tired of his duty and that if he left the soldiers would not have any leadership left at all.[72]

The interrogation also implied that Lang wanted to welcome the foreign expedition at the border.

Asked if, when he had spoken with His Lordship when he last came to the city, he hadn't shown a great urgency to return right away, pretending to be needed at St. Marys; and when His Lordship asked him to stay until the arrival of [Abner] Hammond, which the message brought by the defendant [Lang] suggested would be by the 15th, allowing the defendant to take the necessary action, he hadn't still insisted on being dispatched right away, and that he didn't agree to stay until he heard Captain Hall, who also witnessed the conversation, and who offered to tarry there himself:

He said what the question implies is not true; and that the reason he wanted to leave was that he was needed at home; and that Hall, having offered to stay and His Lordship having told him he [Lang] could go, he nevertheless offered to stay in order to return accompanied by Hall, with whom he had come, for any delay could not be too long because Hammond was soon to arrive.[73]

THE EAST FLORIDA COUNCIL of war decided "in consideration of the small number of cells this fortress has, of the war supplies that they contain, of the fact that they must be used for housing troops in case of the attack that is expected, and that five cells are now occupied by prisoners, there should now be sent to Havana both Abner Hammond and John MacIntosh, who are men of great reputation and power, bringing together the other four in the same cell."[74] Hammond and McIntosh were taken from Castillo de San Marcos on January 28 "with ample escort and custody in the government small boat, with the adjutant of the city, Jose Fernandez, being present for the purpose of transferring then to the sloop *Maria* under Captain Miguel Acosta (then at the point of the bar and ready to receive them and to be underway)."[75] At Havana, McIntosh was confined to a cell in Morro Castle.[76]

UNABLE TO ORGANIZE a legal defense from prison, McIntosh relied on Sarah. She rose to the occasion, as chronicled by Charles Bennett, a decorated World War II veteran, U.S. Congressman and student of Florida history:

> Whether or not the French "rebellion" in Florida had any heroes, there can be no doubt that its heroine was Sarah McIntosh.
>
> Although left with all the responsibilities of the McIntosh plantations, a family of six young children (the oldest was only twelve), and an aged grandmother, she mounted a fervent campaign to free her husband, eventually securing the intervention of President Washington himself.[77]
>
> Her task was made more difficult because an eye infection had left her almost totally blind. She wrote her letters by placing a ruler on the paper and having her children help to guide her hand.[78]

Sarah gathered sworn statements from John's prominent friends and relatives attesting John's character and protesting claims that John had conspired against the East Florida government. John's brother William submitted a statement explaining that Wagnon's trip to Georgia was nothing more than an ordinary business transaction. Not only was he never involved in any plot against East Florida, William said, but also he "reprobated the idea." In fact, William was among the members of the Georgia General Assembly who authorized the Georgia governor to call out the militia to stop "a party of men, which were about to be raised for the purpose of going against East Florida."[79]

Samuel Wright, who served in the General Assembly with William, confirmed that William "was much opposed" to "a party which was about to be raised under the influence of French emissaries," and William "interested himself considerably" in authorizing the militia "to prevent any such party going forward." Wright was "well convinced that neither Col. William McIntosh nor any of his family was ever concerned either directly or indirectly with the said party."[80]

John's uncle Major General Lachlan McIntosh said John "was ever deemed in his private as well as his public character a man of the strictest honor, truth and integrity, whose word as far as he was able was equal to his bond." Noting that John "has taken the oath of allegiance to His Catholic Majesty," Lachlan said "I will wager my life that the whole province would not induce him to forfeit" that oath. When Lachlan had last visited with John and Sarah, "I was astonished to find them both such enthusiastic admirers of the Spanish Government under which they intended to spend their lives."[81]

Josiah Tattnall, Colonel of the Militia of Chatham County, who had been "in the habits of intimacy" with John McIntosh for the past ten years, described him as "an honest and upright man and of the utmost integrity and firm in friendship." During a recent visit, Tattnall had asked McIntosh "how he liked the Spanish government, their customs and practices." McIntosh had replied "that he had found as warm a reception as imaginable, that he was strongly attached to the government and the people, that every privilege possible had been afforded him and others; and finally that he never wished to leave the country." Therefore, "from the well known honesty and integrity" of McIntosh, Tattnall could "hardly believe it possible that he would enter into or be in any wise concerned in conspiracy against the Spanish Government or in any other treasonable act whatever."[82]

The mayor and aldermen of Savannah said McIntosh held "the strictest principles of honor & political integrity, & we conceive that he could not be guilty of so base a conduct as to plot against the welfare of a country from which he has received the highest marks of friendship, confidence and protection." They said they had "never heard the name of Colonel John McIntosh mentioned as being a party" to the proposed illegal expedition, and had never heard of anyone named McIntosh as "being concerned in the business & we verily believe that he has no concern in this matter." The certificate was signed by "W. Stephens, Mayor" and aldermen John Berrien, George Jones, Andrew McCredie, William Lowden, and John Cunningham, who had served as a lieutenant with Elijah Clark in the American Revolution.[83]

Henry Gaither, commander of federal troops in Georgia, certified "that in all conversation I ever had with Col. John McIntosh I never heard him say anything against the Spanish Government and that he always appeared perfectly satisfied with that government; and that I believe him to be a gentleman of strict integrity."[84]

Two officers who had served with Elijah Clark in the American Revolution joined with Lachlan McIntosh, a captain in the United States Army, in declaring:

> ...that during an acquaintance of many years we have known him [John McIntosh] without reproach, either in public or private life; of manners truly inoffensive, we have found him to possess the universal esteem of a numerous and respectable acquaintance in the several circles he has lived. That his mind naturally bent to domestic pursuits suffered him to engage but little in the affairs of government since his retirement from the army; and from what we know of the man we are well assured that nothing could induce him to betray any trust reposed in him or take any measures unfriendly to the interest of the government under which he lived.[85]

The British vice consul for Georgia, John Wallace, certified "that I never heard the name of Colonel John McIntosh mentioned as being concerned directly or indirectly in the Party said to be collecting in this State under the influence of French emissaries with hostile intentions against the flag and territories of His Catholic Majesty. I also certify that I am personally acquainted with Colonel McIntosh and have in no instance had occasion to impeach his honor or integrity, either from my own knowledge of the information of others."

A month passed between the day John was arrested and the time when his friends submitted documents to support him. On March 21, Sarah sent the documents to Governor Quesada. She was informed "that nothing would be done respecting my papers without a formal petition from myself to the Governor, I, in a weak and infirm situation, without loss of time, went to St. Augustine, and on the first day of April, laid a petition before his Excellency, the Governor, praying that the papers already laid before him respecting my husband, Mr. John McIntosh, should be justly translated into the Spanish language."[86]

Sarah received the Spanish translation of the documents on May 25, and immediately sent them to "his Excellency the Captain-General of the Island of Cuba, Louisiana and the two Floridas,"[87] Luis de las Casas.[88] "By those papers," she wrote, "you will be able to judge of the character and connections of my unfortunate husband." Explaining that her husband "unfortunately, though innocently, fell under some suspicion, as I am told, of having views inimical to the government," she followed the course "of candidly laying my unfortunate story before you."

> Is it then reasonable or probable to suppose that a man who for forty years has pursued a life of the strictest honour and most undeviating rectitude, would in a moment descend from every sentiment that was honourable and just, to unite with a set of desperate and unprincipled men, who had nothing to hazard, and whose only views could have been to enrich themselves by the property of others? One who had been for upwards of fourteen months previous to his captivity labouring under a consumptive habit, whose life had several times during that period despaired of by his friends and physicians, with a wife who, I may without vanity say, he most affectionately loved, deprived of sight, and who still is under the influence of the same painfully distressing complaint,

added to all which, the loss of a lovely infant, his only daughter, on whom he doted. Can it, indeed, as I have before observed, be reasonable to believe that a man of such character, in such circumstances and situation, could have designs inimical to a government under which he enjoyed perfect peace and tranquility, his happiness being only disturbed by the afflictions which it has pleased the hand of God to visit himself and his family?

What I have advanced is literally true, and what I can prove readily by my neighbours. To your Excellency's humanity and justice I submit my cause. Justice is all I ask; all I require. Justice from your humane hands I have not a doubt I shall receive; and justice will, I trust, restore my dear partner to his (at present) wretched and disconsolate family. Suffer, O sir! my miserable situation to touch your generous and noble breast with pity and compassion. Allow your imagination to paint my distress to the most lively colours. Imagine you behold before you an unhappy female, deprived of sight, labouring under a continual series of bodily pain, unused hitherto to experience the iron hand of want, whose mental anguish is far the most poignant, with six small children around her, the eldest of whom does not exceed twelve years, with a very slender property to support them, and that daily diminishing for want of its head to direct and manage it to the best advantage. Let me, O sir! for pity's sake, for justice' sake, and for God's sake, entreat you in the most earnest manner to take into consideration my most unhappy case, and as you find no cause for longer detention, restore to liberty your innocent and suffering prisoner, and thereby add new lustre to a character already dignified by acts of liberality, justice and humanity. And what is still more, your generous heart will exult in the pleasing reflection, that you have snatched from misery and ruin an unhappy family, who will to their latest breath feel the highest sense of gratitude for your goodness.

I should be wanting in gratitude to the best of husbands, who ever since our union has reposed the most unbounded confidence in me, did I not declare, that since his residence in this Province, he has been a warm friend, and upwards of two years a faithful servant to the Spanish government, which he served in the office in which he was placed without reward or emolument, to the apparent satisfaction of his superiors, and all others with whom concerned in business.[89]

Months passed and McIntosh remained in prison in Cuba. Sarah wanted to appeal his case to the King of Spain, but bureaucratic red tape stymied her attempts.[90]

Meanwhile, the prisoners held in St. Augustine—William Plowden, Richard Lang, John Peter Wagnon and William Jones—were released after months of captivity. They continued to maintain their innocence and to protest their incarceration and their loss of livelihood. McIntosh's friend Wagnon, who had planned to move and had come to St. Augustine to escort his wife out of East Florida, complained of being "close confined in an uncommon filthy room for three months and twenty-five days, deprived of all sort of communications until the evening of the twenty-ninth of April without ever yet being informed of the cause of his confinement." While he languished in prison, "the little property he has is daily wasting and what is still more distressing a young, tender and affectionate wife reduced to the utmost difficulties."[91]

Sarah McIntosh sent nine letters to her husband during "our painful separation, which God grant, may not be of much longer continuance," although John did not receive all of them. In their correspondence, she learned of his "resignation to the will of Providence, and that you have again recovered your health, for which I am truly thankful; although I must confess I am still fearful respecting your consumptive complaint." She continued, "You flatter me, my dear husband, in saying I would make a good lawyer. I claim no merit; shining abilities are not necessary to plead well in a good cause." Catching him up on family matters, she wrote:

> Agreeably to your desire, I have sent our son William with $100 to his uncle, and requested he should be sent on to New York. My eyes are considerably mended, but as I think Dr. Baron may still be serviceable, I shall, with the Governor's permission, go to Charleston in the course of a fortnight; my stay there I do not expect will exceed more than two months.
>
> I trust, in the goodness of God, the justice of the law, and the humanity of his Excellency the Captain-General, to restore you again shortly to your unhappy family, who all unite in an affectionate remembrance to you.
>
> Adieu, my dear husband, and may the Guardian of innocence protect and restore you to liberty again, is the sincere and daily prayer of your truly affectionate wife,
> Sarah S. McIntosh[92]

Spanish officials in Madrid reviewed the cases against McIntosh and Abner Hammond. The Council of State determined that McIntosh had given moral support to "a conspiracy to invade East Florida from Georgia under French commissions," but did not punish him any further than the time he already had spent in prison.[93] McIntosh either did not receive an explanation of the ruling or did not accept it, and insisted there was no evidence of any crime against him. He declared that he would not "place any faith in a Government that could with impunity thus trample on the common rights of mankind."[94]

When he was released from Moro Castle after eleven months of imprisonment, he had to pay his expenses to travel from Cuba to East Florida. His homecoming took Sarah by surprise.

> On Colonel McIntosh's arrival in Florida, from Cuba, when near his home on the St. Johns, it was announced to his family that he had been released, and would soon be in their midst.
>
> This was a resurrection from the tomb, for all who judged rightly of the injustice and tyranny of this execrable government, believed him lost to his family forever. Mrs. McIntosh sprang from her seat, and with clasped hands expressed the rapturous emotions of her long and sorely-bruised heart in a flood of grateful tears—more eloquent than words.
>
> The tumultuous burst of joy by the family and servants around her was too much for her delicate health, and she sunk upon the floor, oppressed by the overpowering sensations of the moment; and when she awoke to consciousness, found herself in the arms of her husband, whose fate she had so long deplored.[95]

After releasing McIntosh from prison, the Spanish government restored his property and reappointed him as Justice of the Peace on the St. Johns River.[96] While he continued to reside at Bellevue, the Spanish government provided a boat to transport his family to Georgia.[97]

OPEN REBELLION against the Spanish government of East Florida broke out in 1795. Aggressive residents of the southern United States led by General Elijah Clark of Georgia spurred on dissatisfied Anglo setters of East Florida. At the end of June, sixty rebels led by Richard Lang and William Plowden destroyed the Spanish fort at Juana, north of the St. Johns River. The rebels took the garrison as prisoners, and captured a hundred cattle. John McIntosh denied being involved, and offered to help Spanish authorities search for the rebels.[98]

The rebels set up camp just inside the Florida border on Lang's plantation at Mills's Ferry. Spanish officials reported that Lang and Plowden were accompanied by Abner Hammond and expected to be reinforced by a "gang" commanded by Elijah Clark.[99]

Colonel Carlos Howard took precautions against a rebel incursion south of the St. Johns River. McIntosh's plantation at Cowford featured the narrowest crossing place, and Howard depended upon an artillery battery at San Nicolas on the opposite side of the river to guard the crossing.

Howard ordered Captain Timothy Hollingsworth's militia company to patrol a twenty-four mile stretch along the south side of the river on the lookout for invaders. Hollingsworth had to spread his men around, and led a detachment of only six men on the night of July 9. The militiamen stopped at William Lane's plantation downstream from Cowford at 10 p.m., and Lane invited them in for coffee. Lane's brother-in-law arrived and told Hollingsworth that rebels had surrounded the house. Seventy rebels burst through the door and confiscated the weapons of the militia patrol. Lang declared that the militiamen were under house arrest and made them swear that they would not oppose the rebels. When the rebels departed, Lane and his son Pierce accompanied them.[100]

As the rebels proceeded toward the battery at San Nicolas, about thirty East Florida residents joined them. The group included McIntosh and three of the men who had been imprisoned with him the year before: John Peter Wagnon, William Plowden and William Jones.[101] Even if they had been sincere in protesting their innocence in 1794, the hardships they and their families had endured provoked them to rebellion in 1795.[102]

When the rebels reached San Nicolas at 3 a.m. on July 10, one of them spoke to the commander in Spanish and claimed to be with a militia unit sent to reinforce the garrison. Gunfire erupted as more than a hundred rebels attacked the small garrison, killing three Spanish soldiers, wounding several others, and taking twenty-eight prisoners, without any casualties of their own. The rebels then attacked a gunboat anchored in the river at San Nicolas. The crew surrendered after the boat ran aground.

Hollingsworth heard the battle from Lane's house downstream, and when daylight came he went to investigate; he saw a French flag flying from the ramparts of San Nicolas and recognized many of the rebels who had taken him prisoner the night before. Lang sent Hollingsworth to Governor Quesada with a proposal to exchange the garrison of San Nicolas for French personnel who had been taken captive when their ship wrecked on the coast of East Florida.[103]

Spanish officials sent scouts to discover the strength of the rebel force. Luis Maas, who spoke English fluently, infiltrated a rebel victory party at McIntosh's plantation called Cerro Fuente, about six miles downstream from San Nicolas. When Maas arrived at 11:30 p.m. on the evening of the battle, he observed the rebels "drinking, singing, and bragging."[104] Mass reported that "John McIntosh was there in a highly intoxicated condition, vigorously describing his exploits in the successful fray. His boats had been used in the invasion."[105]

Spanish authorities mounted an overwhelming counter-offensive on July 12, and the rebels fled after occupying San Nicolas for only two days. The rebels subsequently set up a stronghold on Amelia Island. Spanish forces from Florida and Cuba drove the rebels from Florida in early August. In October, a Spanish militia captain reported that Clark had gathered a group of rebels, including McIntosh, just inside the Florida border along the St. Marys River. Spanish soldiers attempting to attack the rebels found the rebel camp abandoned. McIntosh, Clark, and the other principal leaders of the rebellion escaped into Georgia.[106]

EUROPEAN WARS and international politics soon drew John McIntosh back into intrigue against the Spanish regime in East Florida. With Spain's grasp on its colonies weakening, Britain feared that France would gain control of Louisiana and the Floridas. British officials, therefore, concocted schemes to seize the colonies from Spain. The British admiralty contacted McIntosh at St. Simons Island in early 1797. McIntosh agreed to recruit volunteers in Georgia who would serve under his command in an expeditionary force to conquer East Florida for Britain; in exchange, the conquerors would receive land in East Florida. McIntosh communicated with the British navy through signals; if he looked out from St. Simons and saw a vessel with "a French ensign at the main topgallant masthead and a Spanish one at the fore," he would answer with "two smokes on shore." Rumors of the intrigue somehow reached Anglo prisoners in St. Augustine, who attempted to escape and join forces with McIntosh.[107] As American sentiment turned against France in international affairs, however, British officials decided to cooperate with the United States on policies affecting East Florida; as a result, the British admiralty never gave McIntosh orders to launch an invasion.[108]

JOHN MCINTOSH RETURNED to East Florida to investigate another rebellion seventeen years after he had fled the province amidst gunfire and conflagration in 1795. General George Mathews, acting as a United States commissioner with covert support from the administration of President James Madison, instigated an uprising of Anglo residents in East Florida who called themselves the Patriots. Coincidentally, John McIntosh's cousin John Houstoun McIntosh emerged as a principal leader of the Patriots. In March of 1812, gunboats of the United States Navy threatened the port of Fernandina on Amelia Island, and the Spanish military commandant surrendered to a force of nearly three hundred Patriots. The next day, Mathews and the Patriots ceded Amelia Island to the United States. The Patriots proceeded to lay siege to St. Augustine, while regular United States troops established a network of outposts stretching from Amelia Island to the vicinity of St. Augustine.[109]

John McIntosh visited the Patriots camp in April "to take a view of the Patriots Camp and to endeavor to form some judgment of the prospects or probability of succeeding in their great object of shaking off tyranny and oppression."[110] He told the United States colonel who commanded the garrisons in East Florida that the

Patriots "would never make much of a fighting force, even as auxiliaries."[111]

Many of the Patriots knew and admired McIntosh, and they pleaded with him to command their army; this posed a dilemma for him because he already held a commission as a major general in the Georgia militia.[112] He explained the situation in a letter to Georgia Governor David B. Mitchell:

> Their little army were determined in a body to elect me their Commander in Chief, which they did unanimously, requesting my acceptance or they would abandon the course they had so warmly espoused. Under such a forcible application I felt myself compelled in some degree to yield up my private ease and interest to their immediate good. I have reluctantly yielded to their request. Should this act be thought incompatible with the Commission I hold in Georgia as Major General of the first Division of Militia, you are at liberty to consider it as vacant and I now tender you my resignation...
>
> I know, my good sir, if you can consistently yield us any support you will do so. I shall be glad to hear from you when your leisure moments will permit...
>
> I enclose you a copy of my Election by the Patriots.[113]

McIntosh attempted to impose discipline on the Patriots. He sentenced a looter, for instance, to a diet of bread and water for eight days.[114] In another instance, a group of Patriots stopped an eleven-year-old boy named Paul Maestre and demanded that he give them his horse. "No," Maestre said, "I will go where my horse goes." The group took him into custody and brought him to their camp. The boy's spirit impressed McIntosh, who released him under condition that Maestre would not fight against the Patriots.

"General McIntosh at that time told me to let him know if any of his people took our property and he would see us righted," Maestre later remembered, "and he told me at the same time that the property of those who fled from their homes and joined the Spaniards would be used and destroyed, but those who remained peacefully in their homes would not be disturbed and if their property was taken that they should have it restored if they complained to him." From then on, Maestre frequently reported property taken from his family by the Patriots, and the property was restored.

The Patriots, Maestre reported, would "plunder and destroy" the property of residents "who quit their places and came to St. Augustine to take up arms against them." When the Maestre family eventually moved out of the war zone, looters raided their plantation and stole provisions, tools, a corn mill, sixty head of cattle, eight horses and thirty-five hogs.[115]

Meanwhile, controversy over the Patriots War embarrassed the Madison administration. The United States government revoked the commission of General Mathews and repudiated the seizure of territory in East Florida by the Patriots. Secretly, however, the administration authorized Governor Mitchell to allow time for events to take shape in East Florida.[116] John McIntosh expressed his dismay over the situation to Mitchell:

> Since writing you last, I find by dispatches from the Seat of Government that General Mathews' operation in East Florida have not met the sanction of the President. This thing is kept a profound secret here. God only knows

what will be the consequences with the unfortunate characters involved in the transaction. I think the government can never abandon them to inevitable ruin, after being in some degree <u>invited</u> to <u>this revolution,</u> and formally ceding the whole Province to the U.S. except the garrison and town of St. Augustine. I find your Excellency has instructions on this head. I hope they are so full as to provide a remedy in this case.

It does, however, appear to me a most extraordinary transaction. I cannot now think of leaving those people while their fate is determined. I therefore anxiously wait your arrival, which we are in hourly expectation of.[117]

Unable to gain support from the United States Senate and the Madison administration, the Patriots faced insurmountable obstacles. Their insurrection ground slowly to a halt as Spanish forces took the offensive and received reinforcements from Cuba. The Patriots eventually withdrew from East Florida.[118]

THE UNITED STATES DECLARED WAR against Great Britain on June 18, 1812, just two months after McIntosh arrived at St. Augustine. Governor Mitchell refused to release McIntosh from his commission as a general in the Georgia militia because a higher duty called: defending the place where he had been born and the nation he had helped to form.[119]

General in the War of 1812

IN THE PIVOTAL CAMPAIGN OF the War of 1812, John McIntosh brought reinforcements to General Andrew Jackson on the coast of the Gulf of Mexico.[1] As a major general in the Georgia militia,[2] McIntosh faced the daunting task of leading 2,500 men hundreds of miles from Georgia to Mobile.[3] He was about sixty years old when he accomplished this strenuous assignment.[4]

Governor Peter Early, as commander in chief of the Georgia militia, designated regiments to rendezvous at Fort Hawkins[5] on the Ocmulgee River by November 21, 1814:

> At Fort Hawkins they will be furnished with provisions by the United States Army Contractor. They will likewise be furnished at the same place with arms and accouterments; but it would be very desirable that all persons who can furnish themselves with rifles, shot-pouches, &c. to do so, as they might be formed into companies of riflemen after their arrival at the rendezvous.
>
> The officers commanding regiments and companies are therefore directed and required to procure as many of this species of arms as possible, because of their great value in the mode of warfare which will in all likelihood be pursued by our enemy. Substitutes may be received, provided they be able-bodied, strong and healthy men, by the captains at or before their arrival at the place of rendezvous, but not after their march from thence.

Major-General John McIntosh and Brigadier-General David Blackshear will command this detachment of militia.[6]

McIntosh told his officers that he expected "good order, and a disposition to forward the interest and welfare of our country, will pervade the army he has the honor to command." Because the Georgia militia units were in federal service, McIntosh noted, "The Rules and Articles of war which govern the United States Army are to be the rule and guide of our conduct."[7] An observer noted "the trouble of managing a large body of raw troops," and said any officer who commands state militia in federal service "and does his duty, fully earns his money."[8]

McIntosh issued orders on November 23 for organizing Blackshear's detachment into two regiments and a battalion. McIntosh also responded to complaints from soldiers about their rations, and authorized Blackshear to appoint "two discreet persons to inspect the beef or pork before it is issued; and should said inspectors reject as unwholesome any part of the rations offered to the troops, the contractor is immediately to be apprized of the same, being his property, that he may make the best disposition he can of any part of the rations legally rejected as unwholesome—the troops having no control over what is not issued to them."[9]

THE WAR OF 1812 against Great Britain erupted on multiple fronts along several borders of the United States. The Savannah government subsequently named city squares commemorating American victories at Chippewa Plains in Canada and New Orleans on the Gulf Coast.[10] John McIntosh's son James Simmons McIntosh served as a lieutenant in the United States Army and in 1813 suffered a severe wound at Black Rock, near the Niagara River in New York State.[11]

A civil war among the Creek Indians became one of the War of 1812's many components. Creeks who fought to protect their territory and their way of life were known as the Red Sticks, while those who chose to assimilate with American culture—including John McIntosh's relative William McIntosh[12]—became allies of General Andrew Jackson. With the help of William McIntosh, Jackson defeated the Red Sticks at Horseshoe Bend in March of 1814. The surviving Red Sticks went into hiding and faced starvation. In the summer of 1814, a party of Royal Marines under Major Edward Nicholls came up the Apalachicola River, established a fort at Prospect Bluff, and assisted the desperate Red Sticks. Jackson directed Major Uriah Blue, commanding a thousand men, to attack the Red Sticks, and ordered General John McIntosh to reinforce Major Blue with enough Georgians to capture the fort at Prospect Bluff. McIntosh consulted with Major William McIntosh and federal Indian agent Benjamin Hawkins about the expedition.[13]

Jackson's orders coincided with Governor Early's desire to attack Seminole Indian settlements near the route to the Gulf. Two weeks after McIntosh and Blackshear gathered their troops at Fort Hawkins, Early obtained what he viewed as permission from Andrew Jackson to attack the Seminoles:

> I have this day written to Gen. McIntosh, and enclosed him a copy of General Jackson's letter to me. This letter contains a paragraph which appears to me to countenance, in a particular manner, the course which was decided on at our conference. The Seminole settlements lying sixty miles to the west of Flint River can, I apprehend, be most advantageously

destroyed by a rapid march from some convenient point on that river, which shall be selected as a depot. The troops may carry provisions enough, without wagons, to last them until their return to the depot. This movement will probably have the advantage, too, of being unexpected by the enemy.

I intend to hold in readiness two hundred horsemen, who will be directed to overtake the infantry, after the latter shall reach the river and establish their first depot. The object will be to co-operate in the destruction of the Seminole settlements.[14]

Under this plan, McIntosh would continue toward Mobile with 1,700 troops, while Blackshear would proceed to the Flint River with a detachment of about eight hundred men. McIntosh put the plan into effect with orders issued on December 14 at Camp Hope near Fort Hawkins:[15]

Brig. Gen. Blackshear will march, with Col. Wimberly's regiment of infantry, direct from this encampment to Hartford, on the Ocmulgee River, and proceed from thence by opening a road in the most direct way to the Flint River, bearing in mind that he must apprize me, from time to time, of the strength and movements of any hostile Indians that he may acquire a knowledge of on his march,—taking special care that the information sent me may be the best his means may afford or admit of, keeping a view of the object of his march—to wit, to deter any hostile or marauding party of Indians from committing acts of violence or making predatory excursions on the frontiers of the State of Georgia most exposed to their savage fury, making every effort at the same time to arrive at the Flint River as speedily as possible, giving me the earliest information of that event.

Upon Gen. Blackshear's arrival at the Flint River, he will proceed to select a proper situation as a place of deposit for provisions, and throw up a small breastwork, with pickets around it, and two block-houses at right angles of the same, about sixteen or eighteen feet square, which will be sufficient to secure the work from assault on every side. A subaltern's command will be sufficient for this station, who will remain and occupy it until otherwise ordered or relieved. His Excellency the Governor will detach two hundred horsemen to join the general at this point, as soon as, in his opinion, a sufficient time has been allowed to this detachment to reach Flint River.

Major Blue, of the 39th Regiment, with about sixteen hundred mounted men, Choctaws, Chickasaws, and Creeks, were to march on the 1st inst. in pursuit of the Red Sticks and their allies. Col. Hawkins's warriors are likewise ready, and will join to chastise the Seminoles or any other hostile tribe of Indians that may be collected or collecting; and (if necessary) I will combine my whole force to that object—which will depend on the intelligence I shall receive from you. If there should be the smallest grounds for believing a collected enemy in the route directed, the general will be particularly cautious to march in regular order, either two or three columns, as he finds most convenient—keeping an advance and rear guard, with double flankers in front, centre, and rear, to prevent surprise or ambuscade. The flankers ought to be relieved every hour, being an arduous duty.

The general's own prudence will suggest the propriety of securing his command from any advantage which the enemy might take in night-attacks, by felling trees and throwing up intrenchments wherever he encamps.

The general will keep in view the importance and necessity of my being well informed in all matters relative to his command, that I may act promptly as circumstances may require; and he will report himself ready to join me as soon as he reaches the Flint River.

Before you march, you will order the regimental surgeon to report to you any of your detachment incapable of performing duty from indisposition; and, should there be any that require medical aid, a surgeon's mate must be left with them, and one or two attendants, if necessary, with orders to proceed on to Fort Mitchell as soon as the surgeon deems them able to perform the march.[16]

Blackshear's troops set out from Fort Hawkins on December 17. They traveled southward roughly fifty miles in four days and arrived at Hartford, where they once again encountered the meandering course of the Ocmulgee River. They could not begin crossing the river until construction crews completed a flat. The crossing operation, "owing to some obstructions," required three days. Two of the first companies to get across began clearing a road and building a bridge over a large creek.

On December 31, Blackshear "decamped from the banks of the Ocmulgee and took up the line of march for Flint River,"[17] a forty-one mile journey[18] that consumed six days. "At this time many of my troops are quite sick;" he told McIntosh, "and, since my departure from Camp Hope, three have died—two here and one on my march; and of hospital-stores I am almost destitute." Blackshear constructed "substantial and durable breastworks" at the Flint River and selected "a proper situation for a fort, and immediately commenced building." [19]

"We seldom have more than one day's forage at a time, and sometimes not that," Blackshear warned McIntosh. "We have no contractor, no soap, none of the component parts of a ration except flour, hogs and salt."[20] The situation got still worse during an attempt to transport five wagons loaded with corn, cartridge boxes and blacksmith tools across the Ocmulgee. "The first wagon got over safe" the assistant forage-master reported, but "the second wagon sunk the flat at the other bank... The wagon is fastened to the bank. The flat has gone down the river. There are some hands after it, but it is uncertain when we will be able to do anything with it."[21] Blackshear scolded the forage-master for mishandling the flat, and ordered him to "lose no time in having the flat brought up and the way made good and safe, and forward on the provisions."[22]

MCINTOSH, MEANWHILE, LED his detachment across the Ocmulgee River at Fort Hawkins on December 27, and began the expedition to Mobile the next morning.[23] The troops marched more than a hundred miles in about nine days to reach Fort Mitchell on the Chattahoochee River.[24] Along the way, McIntosh received a letter written eleven days previously by the commander in Mobile, Brigadier General James Winchester. A British fleet of more than 120 vessels had assembled in the Gulf, Winchester reported, with land forces estimated at six to eight thousand. Winchester expected the British to attack New Orleans first and then Mobile would be the next target. "Therefore permit me to repeat my solicitations for a reinforcement of one or two regiments, to be hastened forward by forced marches," Winchester said. "A few days gained by celerity of movement may insure victory, when without it the conflict may be doubtful."[25]

"No exertion on my part shall be wanting," McIntosh said, "to press forward with all activity, that I can endeavor to be in time to afford my best effort to save our country from the polluted foot of a cruel and oppressive foe."[26] He sent a battalion "to the Tallapoosa, with all the artificers I could collect, to build boats to take us down that river, and the Alabama, to the Mobile, with our provisions—considering this mode as the best I could adopt under existing circumstances, being informed that provisions are not to be had in that quarter, and the want of wagons to convey them any other way compels the alternative."[27]

If he had been aware of the threat to Mobile, McIntosh would not have sent Blackshear's detachment on a detour. McIntosh exclaimed, "I wish to God I had known a month in advance!"[28] A force as large as the one Blackshear commanded was not needed on its present mission, McIntosh said, "as I believe no other enemy is in his route but a few Seminole Indians, not exceeding three hundred, which might have been subdued by one or two companies of foot and a troop of horse." Further, McIntosh had received intelligence that Major Blue had wiped out a Red Sticks encampment, making the expedition to the Apalachicola less urgent. McIntosh wanted Blackshear to proceed to Mobile, but left the decision up to Early as commander in chief of the Georgia militia. "If you think with me, you can give that order positive; otherwise, if you conceive the frontiers of the State of Georgia may be benefited from his services, let him be retained for that service," McIntosh told Early. "I beg that your Excellency will take this broad and discretionary power to govern that business, as my movements will be as rapid as I can make them, without probability of communication with that detachment, or having it in my power of judging of circumstances that might make it necessary to detain them."[29]

Before receiving a reply from Early, McIntosh assumed the emergency would prevent Blackshear's detachment from joining McIntosh's troops. "In consequence of information I have received from Mobile, pressing me to forced marches," McIntosh told Blackshear, "I lamented exceedingly the measure I was advised to, and finally acceded in, of your marching on the east of Flint River to the junction... But, as we are now so far separated that a junction with me to answer the present urgent call at Mobile is entirely impracticable, you will... subdue any hostile tribes of Indians or British in that quarter where Georgia would be affected; and as soon as all disturbances are silenced and overcome by you, you will, without loss of more time than cannot be avoided, march with your command to the support of the Mobile territory, and join me as early as possible."[30]

McIntosh then devised a plan allowing Blackshear's mission to continue while sending part of Blackshear's detachment to Mobile. Under this plan, a thousand allied Indian warriors recruited by federal Indian agent Benjamin Hawkins would assist the troops remaining with Blackshear. "From the overwhelming force that has appeared at New Orleans and Mobile," McIntosh told Blackshear, "Gen. Jackson needs support with all the reinforcements that can possibly be carried to his relief. I fear greatly the enemy will gain some serious advantage. Under these circumstances, I am compelled to call for a battalion from your detachment, as you will have a sufficient number with Col. Hawkins's reinforcement...; and as this detachment was particularly intended for the defense of

Mobile and New Orleans, five hundred detached for the Georgia frontier defense is all I can sanction with the information I am now possessed of." McIntosh ordered Blackshear to "lose not a moment, on receipt of this, in ordering a battalion to join me with all possible expedition. I am told the distance you are now from me does not exceed seventy-five miles."[31]

Governor Early received the letter of General Winchester at Mobile six days after McIntosh forwarded it to him, and was not then aware of McIntosh's plan to divide Blackshear's troops. The next day, Early forwarded the letters of Winchester and McIntosh to Blackshear. "You will perceive by them the imperious necessity for changing your route," Early told Blackshear. "And when I consider the great object for which the War Department required the troops from this State, and when to this view is added the fact, now clearly ascertained, that the very crisis has occurred which was at first only anticipated, I feel a deep conviction that you ought to pursue the original destination of the army." Early ordered Blackshear "to join Gen. McIntosh with the least possible delay."[32]

McIntosh said the governor's decision "evidences his zeal and patriotism for his country's best interest. You will, therefore, without the loss of a moment that can be avoided, press on with your whole detachment agreeable to his orders... Your zeal and patriotism will urge you to every reasonable effort to comply as speedily as you can with this order, which is imperative." McIntosh arranged for a "man well acquainted with the country" to show Blackshear "the best and shortest way you can march your detachment."[33]

Blackshear told McIntosh that operations at the Flint River "were suspended by the reception of dispatches from his Excellency on the evening of the 8th, embracing copies of your letter to him, and from General Winchester to yourself, was well as orders requiring me to retrace my route and pursue you with the utmost expedition."³⁴ The next day, however, Blackshear received the letter McIntosh had written a week earlier "in which you stated the impracticability of our forming a junction," and so continued his march to the Flint River. Two days later, Blackshear received McIntosh's orders "directing me to march with my whole force, in obedience to his Excellency's orders... I shall immediately retrace my steps and take your road at Fort Hawkins, which route I deem it best to pursue from a want of provisions."³⁵

"Gen. McIntosh has gone on to Mobile, and left an imperious order for me to pursue him," Blackshear complained in a private letter to Early, while "the citizens of Georgia may be scalped with impunity." ³⁶

Two days after ordering Blackshear to join McIntosh, the governor changed his mind based on new intelligence from the Georgia frontier. By then, Early seemed aware of the plan to divide Blackshear's troops, and said "I differ with him in believing, according to this state of things, that a battalion would be sufficient; and we have occasion to rejoice that this intelligence has been received so soon after you had orders to retrograde." Early ordered Blackshear "to pursue the route you were going."³⁷

Suddenly, on January 19, 1815, Early gave Blackshear new orders:

> A great crisis in our State has occurred, which has determined me to assume a responsibility in relation to yourself and the regiment under your command, which no other condition of things would justify.

Our State is actually invaded by the enemy, in large force. It is invaded in its most vulnerable point. I have official intelligence that two ships-of-the-line, seven frigates, and a number of smaller vessels have entered St. Andrews' Sound, made a landing on Cumberland Island, and are there establishing themselves. I have further intelligence that their barges occupy all the sounds and inlets between St. Marys and Brunswick, inclusive.

The defense of our own land is the first and most imperious duty. Were the regiment under your command without the State, on its route to Mobile, I should not interfere with it; but, under existing circumstances, I should think it criminal inattention to my own greatest duty to suffer the force to pursue its destination. You are already in the field, prepared at all points, and at the very spot most favorable for marching to the relief of the sea-coast. Before other troops could be collected, organized, and marched there, insurrection on one side, and Indian massacre on the other, may have produced their full measure of ruin. The enemy have black troops with them.

Under all these circumstances, I take on myself the responsibility of ordering you with the force under your command to shape your course, without delay, to the point invaded. You shall hear from me further on your march. Your route, I presume, will be down the river-road through Telfair, across the Oconee at Bell's Ferry, and then to Fort Barrington [on the Altamaha River upstream of Darien]...

I shall, by express, immediately inform Gen. McIntosh of the step I have taken, and transmit to him a copy of this letter.[38]

In a show of respect for the chain of command, Blackshear informed McIntosh as his commanding officer that "without the least intention or inclination to deviate from your orders, I have changed my route, fully anticipating your sanction of the proceeding of his Excellency. But, should circumstances so present themselves as to induce you to order to the contrary, I am still ready cheerfully to obey, and hope your conclusion will be that, if I have erred, it was with the purest intentions, which could only be resisted by a man less attached to his country's interests."[39]

Before receiving the letters from Early and Blackshear about the invasion of Georgia, McIntosh expected Blackshear's detachment to rendezvous with his forces at Fort Decatur on the Tallapoosa River. He informed Blackshear in a letter dated January 22:

> I arrived at this station today with the balance of my detachment from Fort Mitchell. Colonel Boothe, who had the superintendence of building boats for the transportation of the army down this river and the Alabama, has exerted himself beyond my expectation, and in eight or ten days will have sufficient boats to convey fifteen hundred men, baggage and provisions, to Mobile.
>
> I hope that before that period you will have joined us. As it is all-important that you should make use of every effort to accomplish a junction with me, the artificers with you will very much accelerate our object of speedy departure from this place; and a few days gained may afford us an opportunity of rendering essential services to our invaded country.
>
> We learn that General Jackson has for several days been skirmishing with the enemy near Orleans, and that he has

uniformly had the superiority, although with a far inferior force.

It will be necessary for you to send as many pioneers in advance of your army from Fort Bainbridge to this place as you can furnish with tools, to repair the road for your wagons. It was with the greatest difficulty I got on, the road being the worst I ever saw.[40]

The next day, McIntosh wrote again to Blackshear, stressing "the necessity of pressing forward with all diligence—which if you do, I hope you will join me at the Tallapoosa, Fort Decatur, on the 5th or 6th February, when I expect to be ready to take my departure in boats to Mobile. If you should not arrive at that period, I shall be at a loss to give you instructions, as I should, in that event, consider the services of the detachment under your command lost to the General Government."[41]

When McIntosh eventually learned on January 28 that Blackshear's detachment had been recalled, he assured Governor Early that he supported the emergency decision. Freed from the need to wait on Blackshear to catch up with him, McIntosh planned to proceed to Mobile the next morning.[42]

McIntosh continued toward Mobile and covered nearly 150 miles in eleven days.[43] On February 8, he reached Fort Claiborne on a 150-foot-high limestone outcropping overlooking the Alabama River. Fewer than ninety miles stretched between McIntosh and his destination at Mobile,[44] but logistical problems hindered his progress. He immediately apprised General Winchester in Mobile of his situation:

I arrived a few hours ago with part of my detachment by forced marches from Fort Decatur bringing with me provisions for ten days only, leaving a Battalion under the command of Col. Boothe, who was to set out a few days after me in large boats, which I had built for the conveyance of provisions to Mobile for the detachment under my command and was to be supplied by him at this place to enable me to continue on my march. His not having arrived leaves me in a dilemma, and I have no alternative but to wait. Carrying provisions by land I found would have been impracticable even had I been supplied with wagons, which, however, was not the case.

Had I known before I left Georgia the scarcity of provisions at Mobile, and had received any instructions on that head, I would have provided amply...

One regiment of my command was detained by the Governor of the State of Georgia in consequence of a sudden invasion of the enemy in different quarters of the Seaboard, from the County of Camden, to the Southward, including some distance to the north. This enemy has made a landing at two points.[45]

After receiving a letter from McIntosh dated February 11, General Jackson replied he was "happy you are so near Mobile as to reinforce Genl Winchester."[46] Because General Winchester wished to resign, McIntosh assumed command of the Eastern District of the 7th Military District with headquarters in Mobile in mid-February.[47] Provisioning the troops continued to present problems, and when an aide to Jackson visited Mobile, McIntosh told Jackson "The Major can inform you the state he found this army in for want of supplies; although every means that could be devised have been adopted to remedy the evil."[48]

WHILE MCINTOSH ATTEMPTED to reach Mobile, momentous events occurred in Georgia and on the Gulf Coast. In Georgia, British invaders established a beachhead at Cumberland Island on January 11, 1815. On January 13, they forced the American garrison to abandon Point Petre near St. Marys and take up a defensive position on the Altamaha River. St. Marys surrendered to British soldiers who looted the town and its cotton warehouses. The British then burned most of the buildings on St. Simons Island and Jekyll Island. Panic struck the residents of Savannah as the invasion moved up the coast. Peter Early, a former militia officer who served as commander in chief of Georgia militia in his capacity as governor, came from the capital at Milledgeville to Savannah with two thousand soldiers. The British government called off the invasion, and the troops settled in at Cumberland Island. British soldiers who ventured inland blundered into a surprise attack near Coleraine on February 24 and suffered 130 casualties.[49]

On the Gulf, Andrew Jackson won a stunning victory over British invaders approaching New Orleans on January 8. The British then targeted Mobile, which was McIntosh's destination. Brigadier General James Winchester realized that his isolated army at Mobile faced a grave threat. Crews improved the roads leading out of Mobile, ostensibly to improve supply routes but probably to prepare for evacuation. British forces laid siege to Fort Bowyer—at the mouth of Mobile Bay, nearly thirty miles by water from Mobile—on February 9, and the garrison surrendered three days later. Because Winchester failed to hold Fort Bowyer, he announced his resignation and planned to turn over command to McIntosh, whose arrival was overdue and expected any day. Mobile was saved when the British attackers received word that peace had been negotiated between the United States and Great Britain. The British Parliament had ratified a peace treaty in the closing days of 1814, the United States Senate ratified it on February 16, 1815, and the war ended—officially but theoretically—on February 18.[50]

At the 7th Military District Headquarters in New Orleans, General Jackson learned of "prospects of peace" from the British commander on the Gulf. "But as hostilities are not to cease until the treaty is ratified," Jackson instructed McIntosh on February 22, "we are to be vigilant and ready to meet the enemy at all points. Should he have the temerity to advance to Mobile, it is expected you will wipe from the American character the stain occasioned by the capitulation of Fort Bowyer—the enemy must be rejected." Jackson exhorted McIntosh's troops to show "the pride and feelings of freemen."[51]

In a letter to McIntosh dated March 13, Jackson reported that he had "received notice of the ratification of the treaty between the United States and Great Britain, one article of which stipulates for the restoration of all conquests on both sides, I have... received the surrender of the places now in possession of the British forces at or near Mobile Bay." Jackson asked McIntosh to cooperate with British officers "as may be necessary to effect this objective."[52]

McIntosh mentioned "hesitating points with the Commanding Officers of his Britannic Majesty's forces to comply with the article which stipulates a surrender of all conquests on both sides" when he replied to Jackson on March 19. "Should I receive intelligence from the British Commander of his being officially informed of the ratification, I shall immediately be ready to occupy Fort Bowyer, ordering an inventory taken of Ordnance, & the condition received."

McIntosh closed his letter with an indication of personal respect toward Jackson: "Should an opportunity ever be afforded me of rendering you the smallest Services in Georgia, permit to solicit the pleasure of doing so." [53]

The end of hostilities meant that the Georgians who had spent three months marching to Mobile were no longer needed and faced the long trip home. "By the orders received from the Secretary of war," Jackson informed McIntosh, "all the militia are immediately to be discharged—You will therefore hold those under your command in readiness to receive their final discharge." Jackson promised to supply "as much provision as can be spared."[54]

After the militia returned home, the Georgia legislature adopted a resolution thanking "Major-General McIntosh and Brigadier-General Blackshear, and the brave officers and soldiers under their command" for the "the gallant and determined manner" in which they "promptly marched in the most inclement season to meet the enemy," displaying "a zeal and patriotism highly honorable to this army."[55]

The city council of Savannah also adopted resolutions thanking McIntosh for his service. "You had devoted the vigor of manhood in combatting for the liberty and independence of your country," Savannah Mayor Thomas U.P. Charlton wrote to McIntosh in June, "and when that liberty was again menaced by the same foe, an advanced period of life did not prevent you from again unsheathing the sword of seventy-six in defense of the same righteous cause. This consistent patriotism and bravery of conduct exhibits the true features of a character in which love of country and freedom predominates over every other consideration." [56]

Biographical Information

SAVANNAH HISTORIAN Thomas Gamble wrote a brief biographical sketch of John McIntosh in 1923 and concluded: "Too little is known by the present generation of this heroic Georgian."[1] A century later, some details of McIntosh's life no doubt await discovery in history archives, family lore or period newspapers, and some details may not be recorded at all.

Georgia historians agree that McIntosh was born in 1748,[2] while authorities on the American Revolution give his birth date as 1755.[3] The 1755 date appears to be correct, because he swore he was thirty-eight years old in a deposition dated January 23, 1794.[4] He was the first child of William McIntosh, who was the first child of John Mackintosh Mor, who led families from the Highlands of Scotland to Georgia, where they founded Darien. William married Jeanne or Mary Jane Mackay, daughter of James and Barbara Mackay. In addition to John, they had the following children: Lachlan, born in 1750; William, 1752; Margery, 1754; Barbara, about 1760; Hester, 1765; and Donald, 1772.[5]

John's father William became wealthy as a planter in the Darien district, and presumably provided amply for his children. John's correspondence demonstrates an impressive vocabulary, and his brother Lachlan "was a beautiful public speaker and a fine writer for an unlettered region,"[6] lending credence to the family tradition that private tutors educated William's children.[7]

William built a house at Fair Hope on the Sapelo River in the Darien district in the late 1750s or early 1760s, and it later became the home of his son John.[8] John McIntosh was granted forty acres on Patterson Island (south of present-day Valona) in the Darien district in 1771.[9]

John's sister Margery married James Spalding of Sapelo Island in 1772 and became the mother of Thomas Spalding.[10]

The same Revolutionary War authorities who say John McIntosh was born in 1755 say that he became an officer in the Georgia line of the Continental Army in 1775, which is possible because the Continental Congress authorized a battalion in Georgia on November 4, 1775, but not probable because the battalion was not organized until January of 1776. John McIntosh became a captain in the 1st Georgia Regiment on January 7, 1776, under the command of his uncle Lachlan McIntosh. John was promoted to major in September of 1776 and was promoted to lieutenant colonel commanding the 3rd Battalion of the Georgia Continental Line on April 1, 1778.[11] His exploits in the Revolution are detailed in the body of this book.

John's first cousin, thrice removed, Captain William McIntosh, served as a captain in the British army and as an emissary to the Creek Indians during the American Revolution. William and a Creek woman had a son named William, who as an adult became an ally of John McIntosh in the War of 1812. After the Revolution, the British captain married John's sister Barbara, transforming the wartime foes into peacetime brothers-in-law.[12]

John McIntosh married Sarah Swinton on June 17, 1781, in Colleton County, South Carolina. Their children include: William Jackson McIntosh, born in 1782; John Nash McIntosh, born in Liberty County, Georgia, on December 30, 1783; James Simmons McIntosh, born on June 19, 1787, probably in Liberty County; Alexander S. McIntosh, born in about 1788; and George Baillie McIntosh, born in 1789.[13]

During the 1780s, John McIntosh served for several years in the Georgia General Assembly, and served as Sheriff of Chatham County.[14]

McIntosh received a commission as a major in the Glynn County Militia in 1790.[15]

John brought his wife Sarah and their six children to a plantation on the St. Johns River in Spanish East Florida in about 1791.[16] In 1794, John was arrested on suspicion of activities against the Spanish government, and was imprisoned in Havana for about a year.[17] When open rebellion against the Spanish government of East Florida broke out in 1795, McIntosh participated in the capture of Fort San Nicolas.[18] His role as a rebel in Spanish East Florida is detailed in the body of this book.

The Georgia legislature created McIntosh County on December 19, 1793, and John McIntosh's house at Fair Hope on the Sapelo River provided office space for county officials until a courthouse was constructed at Sapelo Bridge.[19] Fairhope probably was uninhabited, because McIntosh was a resident of East Florida at the time.

After escaping from East Florida, McIntosh resumed his career as a planter on the Georgia coast. John and Sarah McIntosh and their children settled on St. Simons Island, where his parents had established themselves after the Revolution.[20] An 1801 map shows "Col. John McIntosh's Lands" near Frederica.[21]

Sarah battled health problems for many years, and she died in 1799 on St. Simons Island.

John then married the widow of William Stevens in Liberty County in September of 1799.[22] John later married Agnes Hightower Hillary, the widow of Revolutionary War officer and Georgia statesman Christopher Hillary.[23]

John McIntosh represented Glynn County in the Georgia Senate in 1804.[24] An undated list shows that McIntosh served on the Glynn County Grand Jury.[25]

An 1802 survey shows land belong to Colonel John McIntosh and to the estate of his father on the Cow Horn Road that loops from Darien to Sapelo Bridge. The survey describes "Land called the Cottage, belonging to the Estate of Col. William McIntosh, Deceased."[26]

John McIntosh served as a Justice of the McIntosh County Inferior Court in 1808.[27] He served on the McIntosh County Grand Jury in the March term of 1811.[28]

The legislature elected McIntosh in 1809 to serve as major general of the 1st Division of the Georgia militia. [29] In an epic journey starting in the autumn of 1814 and ending in the spring of 1815, McIntosh brought reinforcements to General Andrew Jackson on the coast of the Gulf of Mexico. He was about sixty years old when he accomplished this strenuous assignment.[30] The expedition is described in the body of this book.

Several of McIntosh's sons carried on the family's military tradition. George Baillie McIntosh held the appointment of aid-de-camp to his father in the southern division of the Georgia militia at the time he died of an illness in 1813 at age twenty-four.[31] James Simmons McIntosh was wounded in the War of 1812 and received a mortal wound in 1847 while leading a brigade at Molino del Rey, Mexico.[32]

William Jackson McIntosh (1782-1863) served as a lieutenant in the United States Navy; he resigned from the navy in 1808 and married Maria Hillary (1788-1862) of South Carolina. He became one of the most successful planters in Liberty and McIntosh counties in the 1830s and 1840s. Tax records showed he owned 71 slaves and 2,523 acres in the Sapelo River area, including the ancestral McIntosh plantation at Fair Hope. He moved to Savannah in 1846. During the Civil War, he "offered his services to Commodore Josiah Tattnall's Georgia Navy;" he would have been 79 when the war began in 1861.[33]

After the War of 1812, John McIntosh returned to Fair Hope, a plantation on the Sapelo River where he had lived before the Revolution. He resumed his role as a leading businessman and planter in McIntosh County.[34]

John McIntosh served on the first board of directors of the Bank of Darien, which opened in April of 1819.[35]

After the Presbyterian congregation relocated from Sapelo Bridge to Darien, the first full-time Presbyterian minister arrived in 1820, and General John McIntosh was ordained as a ruling elder of the session. [36] Property on Bayard Square that he donated to the church in 1820 was used in 1876 as the site of the church that replaced one destroyed when Union troops burned Darien during the Civil War;[37] accidental fire destroyed the building in 1899 and the present building was constructed on the site in 1900.[38]

The 1825 McIntosh County tax digest shows that John McIntosh of Fair Hope owned 50 slaves and 912 acres of high land.[39] Twenty years later, Jacob Wood sold land including a "tract of 200 acres of pine land bought of William McIntosh, Esquire, as part of the undivided Estate of General John McIntosh."[40]

When McIntosh died in 1826 he was buried in the family cemetery at Fair Hope.[41] The Savannah *Georgian* printed his obituary under the headline "Another Patriot and Warrior of 1776, is no more!!" Although the pressure of newspaper deadlines resulted in a few minor factual errors, the obituary showed great respect:

> With unfeigned regret, we announce to the citizens of this State, the death of General JOHN M'INTOSH — By the Southern mail of last evening, we have received this melancholy intelligence—the communication of this public loss. General M'Intosh was an Officer in the Georgia Line, under the Continental establishment in 1775, and served during the Revolution with unblemished honor, and distinguished patriotism and courage. In 1814, he was again found in the defense of his country, and commanded the Georgia Division, which went to Pensacola, the same patriot and soldier he was in the Revolutionary struggle.
>
> He died at his plantation, in M'Intosh county, near the place of his birth, aged about 70, on Sunday the 12th inst. He expired a sincere christian, amidst sorrowing relatives, friends and neighbors. We have only time to notice this sketch, furnished to us by a friend—A more appropriate tribute to the memory of this worthy, will, no doubt, soon appear before the public.
>
> Noble soul! how the spirit of Washington will greet thee.[42]

A Body in Motion

In 1826 John McIntosh was buried in the family cemetery on a bluff beside the Sapelo River at Fair Hope in McIntosh County, Georgia. Two decades later, a storm washed McIntosh's coffin out of the grave. The family reburied his body in a prestigious type of coffin that had not been invented at the time of his death. The new Fisk coffin was made out of iron and cost a hundred dollars, while a wooden coffin cost only a dollar at that time.

In 2006 a workman trimming bushes for a new owner of Fair Hope found the rusted iron coffin on the bank of the Sapelo River. Evidence proved that the coffin held the remains of John McIntosh. One clue was that the coffin was unusually long, and John was known to have been more than six feet tall, unusually tall for a man in the 1700s.

One of John McIntosh's descendants, Billy McIntosh of Savannah, arranged for John to be buried a third time, and this time farther from the river. John would be buried in the cemetery of another branch of the McIntosh family at Mallow, a plantation adjoining Fair Hope. Billy McIntosh scheduled the third burial of John McIntosh for October 23, 2010. *The Darien News* reported the event:

> On that beautiful October Saturday afternoon, a horse-drawn hearse carried "Col. John" only a mile between his first and second resting place at Fair Hope and what will hopefully be his last, at Mallow.

The glass carriage arrived under a canopy of moss-draped oaks, kicking up dust, as the Savannah Pipe and Drum played "Going Home" on the bagpipes...

Beginning with Billy, the ceremonial shoveling of dirt into the grave began. In the Scottish tradition, flasks containing Scotch whisky were brought out, at which time swigs were taken prior to the pouring of the Scotch over the casket... [1]

The third burial of John McIntosh was a proud moment for his descendants, but it didn't exactly bring what Billy McIntosh's generation might call closure.

"The McIntoshes are so stubborn," Billy McIntosh told *The Darien News*. "He doesn't want to stay in the ground. This may not be the last!"[2]

Photographs

All photos by Daniel McDonald Johnson

View of Medway River from Fort Morris

The Fort Morris State Historic Site at Sunbury, Georgia, marks the spot where John McIntosh, after receiving a summons to surrender the fort, replied, "Come and take it!" The address for the historic site is 2559 Fort Morris Road, Midway, GA 31320, and the GPS Coordinates are N 31.767894 | W -81.281233. The phone number is 912-884-5999.

Fort Morris Historic Site
The earthworks preserved at Fort Morris State Historic Site at Sunbury, Georgia, were built during the War of 1812 on or near the foundations of the Revolutionary War fort where John McIntosh commanded the garrison in November of 1778.

Brier Creek Battlefield Memorial

The Brier Creek Battlefield where John McIntosh was wounded and captured is located in the Tuckahoe Wildlife Management Area; the address is 6199 Brannens Bridge Road, Sylvania, GA 30467, and the GPS Coordinates are N 32.82004, W -81.4834. The phone number is 229-426-5267. The memorial features Georgia marble and the landscaping uses native plants. The visitor shown is a member of the Georgia Society of the Sons of the American Revolution.

View of Brier Creek Swamp

Castillo de San Marcos
The fortress where John McIntosh was interrogated in 1794 is preserved as the Castillo de San Marcos National Monument. The address is 1 South Castillo Drive, Saint Augustine, FL 32084. The phone number is 904-829-6506.

View from the parapet of the Castillo de San Marcos

Mallow Cemetery

The historic Mallow Cemetery where several distinguished members of the McIntosh family are buried is now a public park in Pine Harbor, Georgia, at the intersection of Grouper Lane and Fair Hope Road in McIntosh County about seventeen miles north of Darien. John McIntosh was first buried in 1826 at Fair Hope, which was adjacent to Mallow, and his remains were relocated to Mallow in 2010.

John McIntosh's grave at Mallow Cemetery

View of Mallow Cemetery in Pine Harbor

View of Fair Hope from Mallow

Billy McIntosh

W.S. "Billy" McIntosh, Jr., of Savannah, Georgia, is a descendant of John McIntosh who organized the third burial of John's remains in 2010. He is shown wearing a replica of Continental General Lachlan McIntosh's uniform and standing in front of E. Shaver, Booksellers in Savannah.

Notes

Hero of the American Revolution

[1] Gordon Burns Smith, *Morningstars of Liberty: The Revolutionary War in Georgia 1775-1783* (Milledgeville, Georgia: Boyd Publishing, 2006), 2:170. John McIntosh became a captain in the 1st Georgia Regiment on January 7, 1776, under the command of his uncle Lachlan McIntosh. John was promoted to major in September of 1776 and was promoted to lieutenant colonel commanding the 3rd Battalion of the Georgia Continental Line on April 1, 1778.

[2] Kenneth Coleman, *The American Revolution in Georgia 1763-1789* (Athens: University of Georgia Press, 1958), 107; E. Merton Coulter, *Georgia: A Short History*, 3rd ed. (Chapel Hill: University of North Carolina Press, 1960), 135-36; Martha Condray Searcy, *Georgia-Florida Contest in the American Revolution, 1776-1778* (Tuscaloosa: University of Alabama Press, 1985), 134.

[3] "Order Book of Samuel Elbert, Colonel and Brigadier General in the Continental Army, October 1776 to November 1778," *Collections of the Georgia Historical Society Vol. V, Part 2* (Savannah: The Morning News Print, 1902), 128.

[4] Samuel Elbert to Robert Howe, Frederica, April 19, 1778, quoted in Wm. Berrien Burroughs, "Samuel Elbert," in *Men of Mark in Georgia* (Atlanta: A.B. Caldwell, 1907), 1: 59-60.

[5] Searcy, *Georgia-Florida Contest*, 134-35; Smith, *Morningstars*, 1:104-05.

[6] "Order Book of Samuel Elbert," 128.

[7] Coulter, *Georgia: A Short History,* 136; Searcy, *Georgia-Florida Contest*, 136, 139).

[8] "Order Book of Samuel Elbert," 142.

[9] "Order Book of Samuel Elbert," 149.

[10] Brigade Orders, June 6, 1778, Camp at Reids Bluff, in "Order Book of Samuel Elbert," 162-63.

[11] Searcy, *Georgia-Florida Contest*, 140, 142.

[12] Searcy, *Georgia-Florida Contest*, 144-45.

[13] Searcy, *Georgia-Florida Contest*, 145.

[14] Smith, *Morningstars of Liberty*, 1:107. The officers attending the council of war were: colonels Samuel Elbert, Nicholas Everleigh, Charles C. Pinckney, Robert Rae, John Stirk, Peter Taarling, and John White; lieutenant colonels William Henderson, John McIntosh, Daniel Roberts, and William Scott; and majors William Brown, John Fauchereau Grimke, Romand, John Habersham, Joseph Lane, Thomas Pinckney, and Samuel Wise.

[15] "Order Book of Samuel Elbert," 177.

[16] "Order Book of Samuel Elbert," 178.

[17] Searcy, *Georgia-Florida Contest*, 179-80.

[18] Searcy, *Georgia-Florida Contest*, 161-63.

[19] Searcy, *Georgia-Florida Contest*, 163; Patrick O'Kelly, *Nothing But Blood and Slaughter: The Revolutionary War in the Carolinas, Volume One 1771-1779* (Barbecue, N.C.: Patrick O'Kelly, 2004), 208-10.

[20] Several sources refer to Mark Prevost as a colonel or lieutenant colonel, but Searcy and O'Kelly (cited above) agree that he was a major in November of 1778.

[21] Paul McIlvaine, *The Dead Town of Sunbury, Georgia* (Hendersonville, N.C.: Paul McIlvaine [printed by Groves Printing Co., Asheville, N.C.], 1971), 42; John McKay Sheftall, *Sunbury on the Medway: A Selective History of the Town, Inhabitants and Fortifications* (Atlanta: State of Georgia Department of Natural Resources Office of Planning and Research, Historic Preservation Section, 1977), 36-37. There are slight differences in the punctuation and capitalization.

[22] McIlvaine, *The Dead Town of Sunbury*, 43; R.J. Massey, "John McIntosh," in *Men of Mark in Georgia*, ed. William J. Northen, (Atlanta: A.B. Caldwell, 1907), 242. There are slight differences in the punctuation and capitalization.

[23] Massey, "John McIntosh," 243.

[24] Daniel McDonald Johnson, *Savannah, Augusta & Brier Creek* (Allendale, S.C.: Daniel McDonald Johnson [distributed by Ingram], 2018), 53; George White, *Historical Collections of Georgia* (Baltimore: Genealogical Publishing Company, 1969), 470-74.

[25] Patrick Murray, "Memoir of Major Patrick Murray, Who Served in the 60th from 1770 to 1793," in *The Annals of the King's Royal Rifle Corps, Vol. 1: The Royal Americans*, ed. Lewis Butler (London: Smith, Elder & Co., 1913), 310-11. Describing the second siege of Sunbury in January of 1779, Murray writes:

> …Mr. Roderic Mackintosh accompanied by his faithful Negro Cyrus, disdaining the counsel of Cyrus, walked under the musketry of the Garrison, setting them at defiance, when they shot him down and disarmed him so quickly that Lieutenant Baron Breitenbach and Sergeant Supman of the 4th. Battalion Light Infantry who with alacrity ran to his rescue could only carry him in wounded in the face. As soon as our men seized him the Americans ceased firing…
>
> …a shell fell upon a building where the rebel officers messed, and killed and wounded 9 of them, and shattered about 50 stand of arms; upon which they proposed to capitulate; which being refused and 2 more shells falling into the fort, they hauled down their colours and surrendered at discretion… The Garrison with their

Commander Major Lane embarked for Savannah... Lieutenant Colonel Allen was left at Sunbury with the Jersey Volunteers. Mr. Mackintosh was appointed Captain of the Fort, he lost the use of his eye.

[26] Charles C. Jones, *The Life and Service of the Honorable Major General Samuel Elbert of Georgia*, (1887, Charleston, S.C.: BiblioLife, 2011), 21.

[27] Archibald Campbell, *Journal of an expedition against the rebels of Georgia in North America under the orders of Archibald Campbell Esquire Lieut. Colol. of His Majesty's 71st Regimt. 1778*, ed. Colin Campbell, (Augusta, Georgia: Richmond County Historical Society, 1981), 21.

[28] Campbell, *Journal of an Expedition*, 23-26.

[29] Alexander A. Lawrence, "General Robert Howe and the British Capture of Savannah in 1778," *Georgia Historical Quarterly* 36: 4 (December 1952), 311.

[30] Lawrence, "General Robert Howe and the British Capture of Savannah," 316, 320-21.

[31] Campbell, *Journal of an Expedition,* 28.

[32] Lawrence, "General Robert Howe and the British Capture of Savannah," 324-25; Campbell, *Journal of an Expedition*, 43-44.

[33] *Papers of George Washington, Revolutionary War Series,* ed. Dorothy Twohig, et. al. (Charlottesville, University of Virginia Press, 1985), 18: 578, n. 2.

[34] Campbell, *Journal of an Expedition,* 40.

[35] Campbell, *Journal of an Expedition,* 102, n. 5.

[36] Campbell, *Journal of an Expedition,* 48-49.

[37] David S. Heidler, "The American Defeat at Briar Creek, 3 March 1779," *Georgia Historical Quarterly* 66.3 (Fall 1982), 318.

[38] Edward J. Cashin Jr. and Heard Robertson, *Augusta and the American Revolution: Events in the Georgia Back Country, 1773-1783* (Augusta, Georgia: Richmond County Historical Society, 1975), 26.

[39] Campbell, *Journal of an Expedition*, 49-50, 108 n. 45.

[40] Campbell, *Journal of an Expedition*, 50-52.

[41] Campbell, *Journal of an Expedition*, 53.

[42] Campbell, *Journal of an Expedition*, 54.

[43] Campbell, *Journal of an Expedition*, 54, 120 n. 136.

[44] Campbell, *Journal of an Expedition*, 57-58.

[45] Robert Scott Davis Jr., *Georgians in the Revolution: At Kettle Creek (Wilkes County) and Burke County* (Easley, S.C.: Southern Historical Press, 1996), 90; T.S. Arthur, *The History of Georgia* (Philadelphia: 1852), 157, retrieved online from *Sabin Americana*, Gale, Cengage Learning; Patrick O'Kelley, *Nothing but Blood and Slaughter: The Revolutionary War in the Carolinas* (Barbecue, N.C.: Patrick O'Kelley, 2004), 1: 248, 251.

[46] Campbell, *Journal of an Expedition*, 62-68.

[47] Campbell, *Journal of an Expedition*, 68.

[48] Campbell, *Journal of an Expedition*, 70.

[49] Campbell, *Journal of an Expedition*, 74-75.

[50] David S. Heidler, "The American Defeat at Briar Creek, 3 March 1779," *Georgia Historical Quarterly* 66.3 (Fall 1982), 322; Joshua B. Howard, "'Things here wear a melancholy appearance:' The American Defeat at Briar Creek," *Georgia Historical Quarterly* 88.4 (Winter 2004), 486, 490.

[51] John C. Dann, *The Revolution Remembered: Eyewitness accounts of the War for Independence* (Chicago: University of Chicago Press, 1980), 177.

[52] Heidler, "The American Defeat at Briar Creek," 322-23.

[53] Dann, *The Revolution Remembered*, 177; Heidler, "The American Defeat at Briar Creek," 324-25.

[54] Heidler, "The American Defeat at Briar Creek," 323.

[55] Heidler, "The American Defeat at Briar Creek," 325; William Moultrie, *Memoirs of the American Revolution*, (New York: The New York Times & Arno Press, 1968), 1: 341; David K. Wilson, *The Southern Strategy: Britain's Conquest of South Carolina and Georgia, 1775-1780* (Columbia: University of South Carolina Press, 2005), 94.

[56] William Gordon, *The history of the rise, progress, and establishment, of the independence of the United States of America: including an account of the late war* (London: printed for the author, 1788), 3:233; Frank Moore, *Diary of the American Revolution from Newspapers and Original Documents* (New York: The New York Times & Arno Press, 1969), 2: 141 n.

[57] Heidler, "The American Defeat at Briar Creek," 325; Wilson, *The Southern Strategy*, 94.

[58] Heidler, "The American Defeat at Briar Creek," 328; Wilson, *The Southern Strategy*, 98-99; Moultrie, *Memoirs*, 1: 340-42.

[59] Dann, *The Revolution Remembered*, 179.

[60] Heidler, "The American Defeat at Briar Creek," 328-29.

[61] Campbell, *Journal of an Expedition*, 77.

[62] Heidler, "The American Defeat at Briar Creek," 328-29; Wilson, *The Southern Strategy*, 96; Dann, *The Revolution Remembered*, 179.

[63] Francis B. Heitman, *Historical Register of Officers of the Continental Army* (Washington: The Rare Book Shop Publishing Company, 1914), 213, 371; Wilson, *The Southern Strategy*, 96.

[64] Dann, *The Revolution Remembered*, 181.

[65] Heidler, "The American Defeat at Briar Creek," 330; Wilson, *The Southern Strategy*, 96; Howard, "'Things here wear a melancholy appearance,'" 494.

[66] Dann, *The Revolution Remembered*, 181.

⁶⁷ William Moultrie, *Memoirs of the American Revolution*, (New York: The New York Times & Arno Press, 1968), 1: 324-25.

⁶⁸ Dann, *The Revolution Remembered,* 181.

⁶⁹ Enoch Autry, "In honor of Revolutionary War patriots," *The Sylvania Telephone* 10 October 2019, 8.

⁷⁰ K.G. Davies, *Documents of the American Revolution, 1770-178* (Shannon: Irish University Press, 1972), 17: 78.

⁷¹ Moultrie, *Memoirs*, 1: 326.

⁷² The American officers captured at Brier Creek were paroled at Sunbury during the summer and fall of 1779. The officers on parole could rent residences, find employment, and sometimes travel to Savannah. When British forces abandoned Sunbury in September to reinforce Savannah, the American officers became vulnerable to marauding loyalists, who succeeded in killing one Continental captain. The American officers also suffered from scarcities of food and supplies. In the aftermath of the disastrous Siege of Savannah, American forces withdrew into South Carolina and Continental General Benjamin Lincoln advised the officers at Sunbury to move to safety while still being considered prisoners of war on parole. By October, all of the officers had left Sunbury. See: John McKay Sheftall, *Sunbury on the Medway: A Selective History of the Town, Inhabitants and Fortifications* (Atlanta: State of Georgia Department of Natural Resources Office of Planning and Research, Historic Preservation Section, 1977), 47-52, 135. Sheftall does not include John McIntosh among the officers paroled at Sunbury, which could be simply an omission or could indicate that McIntosh was not at Sunbury.

Perhaps McIntosh was sent to Savannah to be treated for the wound he incurred at Brier Creek, because he later defended a loyalist doctor who was accused of mistreating prisoners; McIntosh attested to the doctor's "humanity and attention to the sick, wounded, and distressed American prisoners and families whilst under the British domination at or near Savannah." See: *Georgia Citizen Soldiers of the American Revolution,*

1979, ed. Robert S. Davis, Jr. (Greenville, S.C.: Southern Historical Press, 2000), 56-57.

In May of 1780, McIntosh was in Augusta. He was exchanged sometime after June of 1780 for Lieutenant Colonel John Harris Cruger. See: Smith, *Morningstars*, 2: 170.

[73] Massey, "John McIntosh," 243; Mark M. Boatner III, *Encyclopedia of the American Revolution* (New York: David McKay Company, 1976), 692; Lilla M. Hawes, ed., "The Papers of James Jackson 1781-1798," *Collections of the Georgia Historical Society Vol. XI* (Savannah: Georgia Historical Society, 1935), 19.

[74] Smith, *Morningstars*, 2: 170.

[75] George White, *Historical Collections of Georgia,* 1854 (Danielsville, Ga.: Heritage Papers, 1968), 547-48.

John and Sarah married on June 17, 1781, in Colleton County, South Carolina. Their first child was born in 1782. See: Smith, *Morningstars*, 2: 170-71.

[76] Robert Baillie to Lachlan McIntosh, St. Augustine, July 17, 1781, *Papers of Lachlan McIntosh,* ed. Lilla M. Hawes: Georgia Historical Society, 1957), 98.

[77] Baillie to McIntosh, July 17, 1781, in *Papers of Lachlan McIntosh,* 99.

[78] Statement of Lachlan McIntosh, Savannah, Feb. 22, 1794, in Charles E. Bennett, *Florida's "French" Revolution 1793-1795* (Gainesville: University Presses of Florida, 1981), 140.

[79] Statement of Lachlan McIntosh, Feb. 22, 1794, in Bennett, *Florida's "French" Revolution*, 140.

Rebel in East Florida

[1] Charles E. Bennett, *Florida's "French" Revolution 1793-1795* (Gainesville: University Presses of Florida, 1981), 12-13; White, *Historical Collections of Georgia,* 551.

[2] Charles E. Bennett, *Florida's "French" Revolution 1793-1795* (Gainesville: University Presses of Florida, 1981), 139.

[3] Charles E. Bennett, *Florida's "French" Revolution 1793-1795* (Gainesville: University Presses of Florida, 1981), 12-13.

[4] Cormac A. O'Riordan, "The 1795 Rebellion in East Florida" (1995), *University of North Florida Graduate Theses and Dissertations* No. 99, https://digitalcommons.unf.edu/etd/99, 4-5.

[5] O'Riordan, "1795 Rebellion," 67.

[6] O'Riordan, "1795 Rebellion," 68.

[7] O'Riordan, "1795 Rebellion," 70.

[8] O'Riordan, "1795 Rebellion," 70.

[9] O'Riordan, "1795 Rebellion," 60.

[10] Rembert W. Patrick, *Florida Fiasco: Rampant Rebels on the Georgia-Florida Border, 1810-1815* (Athens: University of Georgia Press, 1954), 51-52; Rembert's source is the Scrapbook of T. Frederick Davis in the Yonge Library of Florida History at the University of Florida.

[11] O'Riordan, "1795 Rebellion," 53.

[12] O'Riordan, "1795 Rebellion," 64-65.

[13] O'Riordan, "1795 Rebellion," 74-75.

[14] O'Riordan, "1795 Rebellion," 76.

[15] O'Riordan, "1795 Rebellion," 75-76.

[16] O'Riordan, "1795 Rebellion," 118 n. 51

[17] O'Riordan, "1795 Rebellion," 77.

[18] O'Riordan, "1795 Rebellion," 79-80.

[19] George White, *Historical Collections of Georgia,* 1854 (Danielsville, Ga.: Heritage Papers, 1968), 551.

[20] Bennett, *Florida's "French" Revolution*, 136.

[21] White, *Historical Collections of Georgia,* 548-49.

[22] Bennett, *Florida's "French" Revolution*, 84.

[23] Bennett, *Florida's "French" Revolution*, 141.

[24] Bennett, *Florida's "French" Revolution*, 140.

[25] Bennett, *Florida's "French" Revolution*, 22-24.

[26] Bennett, *Florida's "French" Revolution*, 27-29.

[27] Bennett, *Florida's "French" Revolution*, 29.

[28] Bennett, *Florida's "French" Revolution*, 33.

[29] Bennett, *Florida's "French" Revolution*, 33-44.

[30] Bennett, *Florida's "French" Revolution*, 81-82, 85.

[31] Bennett, *Florida's "French" Revolution*, 139.

[32] Bennett, *Florida's "French" Revolution*, 110.

[33] Bennett, *Florida's "French" Revolution*, 63.

[34] Bennett, *Florida's "French" Revolution*, 110.

[35] Bennett, *Florida's "French" Revolution*, 108.

[36] Bennett, *Florida's "French" Revolution*, 108.

[37] Bennett, *Florida's "French" Revolution*, 81.

[38] Bennett, *Florida's "French" Revolution*, 71.

[39] Bennett, *Florida's "French" Revolution*, 124.

[40] Bennett, *Florida's "French" Revolution*, 121.

[41] Bennett, *Florida's "French" Revolution*, 119.

[42] Bennett, *Florida's "French" Revolution*, 47-55.

[43] Bennett, *Florida's "French" Revolution*, 119.

[44] Bennett, *Florida's "French" Revolution*, 124.

[45] Bennett, *Florida's "French" Revolution*, 79.

[46] Bennett, *Florida's "French" Revolution*, 56.

[47] Bennett, *Florida's "French" Revolution*, 129.

[48] Bennett, *Florida's "French" Revolution*, 79.

[49] Bennett, *Florida's "French" Revolution*, 79-80.

[50] Bennett, *Florida's "French" Revolution*, 103.

[51] Bennett, *Florida's "French" Revolution*, 51.

[52] Bennett, *Florida's "French" Revolution*, 52.

[53] Bennett, *Florida's "French" Revolution*, 108.

[54] Bennett, *Florida's "French" Revolution*, 102.

[55] Bennett, *Florida's "French" Revolution*, 122.

[56] Bennett, *Florida's "French" Revolution*, 99.

[57] Bennett, *Florida's "French" Revolution*, 168.

[58] Bennett, *Florida's "French" Revolution*, 168.

[59] Bennett, *Florida's "French" Revolution*, 23, 81, 84.

[60] White, *Historical Collections of Georgia*, 553.

[61] Bennett, *Florida's "French" Revolution*, 84.

[62] Bennett, *Florida's "French" Revolution*, 76.

[63] O'Riordan, "1795 Rebellion," 95-96.

[64] Bennett, *Florida's "French" Revolution*, 78-79.

[65] Bennett, *Florida's "French" Revolution*, 81.

[66] Bennett, *Florida's "French" Revolution*, 81.

[67] Bennett, *Florida's "French" Revolution*, 79, 81.

[68] Bennett, *Florida's "French" Revolution*, 82.

[69] Bennett, *Florida's "French" Revolution*, 82-83.

[70] Bennett, *Florida's "French" Revolution*, 83.

[71] Bennett, *Florida's "French" Revolution*, 121-22.

[72] Bennett, *Florida's "French" Revolution*, 121.

[73] Bennett, *Florida's "French" Revolution*, 121.

[74] Bennett, *Florida's "French" Revolution*, 77.

[75] Bennett, *Florida's "French" Revolution*, 97-98.

[76] Bennett, *Florida's "French" Revolution*, 137.

[77] Bennett's source is George White, *Historical Collections of Georgia*, 549: "…the private influence of General Washington, and of the most distinguished men of our country, many of who had served with him [John McIntosh] during the war, was exerted in his behalf, mainly through the active correspondence and ceaseless efforts of Mrs. McIntosh;" White does not give his sources. A search of *The Papers of George Washington, Presidential Series*, ed. Dorothy Twohig and others (Charlottesville: University Press of Virginia, 1987 and ongoing) does not discover any reference to John McIntosh's plight, but that does not preclude "private influence." Washington did correspond with John's uncle Lachlan McIntosh, who had served with Washington at Valley Forge. Also, the officer selected by Washington to command federal troops in Georgia did submit a statement of support for John McIntosh (see Bennett, 146).

[78] Bennett, *Florida's "French" Revolution*, 136.

[79] Bennett, *Florida's "French" Revolution*, 139.

[80] Bennett, *Florida's "French" Revolution*, 146.

[81] Bennett, *Florida's "French" Revolution*, 140.

[82] Bennett, *Florida's "French" Revolution*, 141-42.

[83] Bennett, *Florida's "French" Revolution*, 142-43.

[84] Bennett, *Florida's "French" Revolution*, 146.

[85] Bennett, *Florida's "French" Revolution*, 144-45.

[86] White, *Historical Collections of Georgia*, 550.

[87] White, *Historical Collections of Georgia*, 551.

[88] Bennett, *Florida's "French" Revolution*, 136.

[89] White, *Historical Collections of Georgia*, 551-52.

[90] White, *Historical Collections of Georgia*, 553.

[91] Bennett, *Florida's "French" Revolution*, 166-70.

[92] White, *Historical Collections of Georgia*, 552-54.

[93] Bennett, *Florida's "French" Revolution*, 166-67.

[94] O'Riordan, "1795 Rebellion," 94.

[95] White, *Historical Collections of Georgia*, 549-50.

[96] O'Riordan, "1795 Rebellion," 93.

[97] Bennett, *Florida's "French" Revolution*, 185, 195-96.

[98] Bennett, *Florida's "French" Revolution*, 177-80.

[99] Bennett, *Florida's "French" Revolution*, 181, 184, 186.

[100] O'Riordan, "1795 Rebellion," 8-10.

[101] Bennett, *Florida's "French" Revolution*, 186.

[102] O'Riordan, "1795 Rebellion," 92.

[103] O'Riordan, "1795 Rebellion," 10-12.

[104] Bennett, *Florida's "French" Revolution*, 190.

[105] Charles E. Bennett, *Southernmost Battlefields of the Revolution* (Bailey's Crossroads, Va.: Blair, 1970), 64.

[106] Bennett, *Florida's "French" Revolution*, 193-98.

[107] J. Leitch Wright Jr., *Britain and the American Frontier, 1783-1815* (Athens: University of Georgia Press, 1975), 112; Bennett, *Florida's "French" Revolution*, 201.

[108] Wright, *Britain and the American Frontier*, 116.

[109] James G. Cusick, *The Other War of 1812* (Athens: University of Georgia Press, 2007), 124-25, xv, 193

[110] John McIntosh to David Mitchell, Patriots Camp before the Walls of St. Augustine, April 27, 1812, Miscellaneous Manuscript Collection at the P.K. Yonge Library of Florida History, University of Florida, call number 00,0433, https://ufdc.ufl.edu/AA00024278/00001/thumbs

[111] Cusick, *The Other War of 1812*, 165.

[112] Cusick, *The Other War of 1812*, 164-65.

[113] John McIntosh to David Mitchell, April 27, 1812, previously cited.

[114] Cusick, *The Other War of 1812*, 196.

[115] Cusick, *The Other War of 1812*, 200-01.

[116] Cusick, *The Other War of 1812*, xv.

[117] John McIntosh to David Mitchell, Patriots Camp, May 1, 1812, Miscellaneous Manuscript Collection at the P.K. Yonge Library of Florida History, University of Florida, call number 00,0433, https://ufdc.ufl.edu/AA00024278/00001/thumbs

[118] Cusick, *The Other War of 1812*, xv-xvi.

[119] Cusick, *The Other War of 1812*, 332 n. 53.

General in the War of 1812

[1] Thomas Gamble, *Savannah Duels and Duelists,* 1923, (Savannah: Oglethorpe Press, 1997), 22. "When the second war came with Great Britain," Gamble wrote, "John McIntosh was called into his country's service again, this time as a general to command three regiments of infantry and a battalion of artillery for the protection of Savannah and the seaboard. When the British threatened the Gulf country General McIntosh with his gallant Georgians, including many Savannahians, marched a thousand miles through the wilderness to the defense of Mobile." The information—including the mileage figure of a thousand miles—was repeated seven years later in Margaret Davis Cate, *Our Todays and Yesterdays* (Brunswick, Ga.: Glover Brothers, revised edition, 1930), 189.

Google Maps says the shortest route from McIntosh's starting point at present-day Macon, Georgia, to Mobile, Alabama, is 353 miles; McIntosh, however, could not follow a direct route in 1814. He went at least 110 miles from Macon to Fort Mitchell, Alabama, next at least 70 miles to Fort Decatur at present-day Milstead, Alabama, then at least 140 miles to Claiborne, Alabama, and finally at least 80 miles to Mobile, for a total of at least 400 miles. Assuming he returned along roughly the same route, his round trip would have been very close to a thousand miles.

[2] Gordon Burns Smith, *History of the Georgia Militia, Vol. 1* (Milledgeville, Ga.: Boyd Publishing, 2000). In a biographical sketch of McIntosh on pages 321-22, Smith reports that McIntosh received a commission as a major in the Glynn County Militia in 1790, and the legislature elected him in 1809 to serve as major general of the 1st Division of the Georgia militia. Page 388 specifies that the 1st Division originally included the counties of Camden, Chatham, Glynn, Liberty, Burke and Effingham, and later covered McIntosh and other counties in the region. Page 148 shows that McIntosh commanded a division of

Georgia militia in federal service from December of 1814 through May of 1815. The division included: the 1st Brigade of Georgia Militia, commanded by Brigadier General John Floyd and stationed at Savannah; the 2nd Brigade, commanded by Brigadier General David Blackshear, ordered to Mobile but diverted to Fort Barrington on the Altamaha River near Darien; and the 4th Regiment, stationed at Fort Decatur. McIntosh, however, was on his mission to Mobile at this time, so the day-to-day command responsibilities in Georgia must have been entrusted to other officers. McIntosh retired on November 1, 1815.

[3] The number of troops—2,500—is given in various sources including Lawton B. Evans, *History of Georgia* (New York: American Book Company, 1898), 177.

[4] Revolutionary War historians say that McIntosh was born in 1755 (see, for example, Boatner, *Encyclopedia of the American Revolution*, 691), but do not give a month or day, so he would have been fifty-nine or sixty when the expedition began in November of 1814 and could have turned sixty-one before the expedition ended in 1815.

[5] The site of Fort Hawkins is in present-day Macon, Georgia.

[6] Gov. Early to Gen. Blackshear, Milledgeville, Ga., Oct. 21, 1814 in *Memoir of Gen. David Blackshear*, included in *The Bench and Bar of Georgia*, ed. Stephen F. Miller (Philadelphia: J.B. Lippincott, 1858), 422. Blackshear's memoir also is available online in the Sabin Americana series published electronically by Gale.

[7] John McIntosh to David Blackshear, (Detachment Orders), November 23, 1814, Fort Hawkins, in *Memoir of Gen. David Blackshear*, 423-24.

[8] Mark Hardin to David Blackshear, November 27, 1814, Camp Covington, in *Memoir of Gen. David Blackshear*, 424.

[9] John McIntosh to David Blackshear, (Detachment Orders), November 23, 1814, Fort Hawkins, in *Memoir of Gen. David Blackshear*, 423-24.

[10] Walter J. Fraser, *Savannah in the Old South* (Athens: University of Georgia Press, 2003), 183.

[11] Smith, *Morningstars*, 2: 171; *Appleton's Cyclopedia of American Biography* v. 3 (New York, 1888, available online from Gale), 124; "Raid on Black Rock," *The War of 1812: The Forgotten War to Save the Republic,* http://theuswarof1812.org/battledetail.aspx?battle=64

[12] Buddy Sullivan, *Early Days on the Georgia Tidewater: The Story of McIntosh County & Sapelo* (Darien: McIntosh County Board of Commissioners, 1990, 36-37. William McIntosh's mother was a Creek woman and his father was an American-born descendant of the McIntoshes who founded Darien. William McIntosh of the Creeks was a great-great-grandson of Brigadier William Mackintosh of Borlum—a commander of Jacobite forces in the Risings of 1715 and 1719—through the Brigadier's natural son Benjamin. See: Iain Moncrieffe and David Hicks, *The Highland Clans,* 1967 (New York: Bramhall House, 1977), 128. John McIntosh was a great-grandson of Lachlan Mackintosh of Knocknagael—a younger brother of Brigadier William McIntosh—through his son John Mackintosh Mor, leader of the Scottish Highlanders who founded Darien. See: "Mackenzie Papers, Part II" ed. Albert S. Britt Jr. and Lilla M. Hawes, *Georgia Historical Quarterly* v.57 no. 1 (Spring 1973), 110-12; William Fraser Ross, "Family of Mackintosh of Borlum," *Clan Chattan* v. 1 no. 6 (1939), 180-90.

[13] *Encyclopedia of the War of 1812,* ed. David S. Heidler and Jeanne T. Heidler (Santa Barbara: ABC-CLIO, 1997), 205-07; David S. Heidler and Jeanne T. Heidler, *Old Hickory's War: Andrew Jackson and the Quest for Empire* (Baton Rouge: Louisiana State University Press, 2003), 47-50; Frank Lawrence Owsley Jr., *Struggle for the Gulf Borderlands: The Creek War and the Battle of New Orleans 1812-1815* (Gainesville: University Presses of Florida, 1981), 174-75. Among Owsley's sources are a letter from Jackson to McIntosh, Nov. 16, 1814, and a letter from McIntosh to Jackson, Dec. Dec. 18, 1814.

[14] Peter Early to David Blackshear, December 9, 1814, Milledgeville, in *Memoir of Gen. David Blackshear*, 426.

[15] The number of troops in McIntosh's detachment—1,700—and the location of Camp Hope—"near Fort Hawkins in central Georgia"—are

given in Billy Lee Atkins, "Georgians and the War of 1812" (1968), Georgia Southern College thesis for Master of Arts in History, 128.

[16] John McIntosh to David Blackshear, (Detachment Orders), January 3, 1815, Hartford, in *Memoir of Gen. David Blackshear*, 426-27.

[17] David Blackshear to John McIntosh, Jan. 11, 1815, Camp, Flint River, in *Memoir of Gen. David Blackshear*, 445.

[18] David Blackshear to Alexander McDonald, January 7, 1815, Camp at Flint River, in *Memoir of Gen. David Blackshear*, 439-40.

[19] David Blackshear to John McIntosh, Jan. 11, 1815, Camp, Flint River, in *Memoir of Gen. David Blackshear*, 445.

[20] David Blackshear to John McIntosh, December 30, 1814, Camp on the west side of Ocmulgee, in *Memoir of Gen. David Blackshear*, 431-32.

[21] Alexander McDonald to David Blackshear, December 14, 1814, Camp Hope, in *Memoir of Gen. David Blackshear*, 426-27.

[22] David Blackshear to Alexander McDonald, January 4, 1815, Camp at Twenty-Six Mile Creek, in *Memoir of Gen. David Blackshear*, 435.

[23] Anthony Forbes to David Blackshear, Dec. 30, 1814, Milledgeville, in *Memoir of Gen. David Blackshear*, 432.

[24] John McIntosh to David Blackshear, Jan. 5, 1815, in *Memoir of Gen. David Blackshear*, 436. The Fort Mitchell Historic Site is in present-day Fort Mitchell, Alabama, 36856. The most direct route from Macon to Fort Mitchell on Google Maps is 109 miles.

[25] James Winchester to John McIntosh, Dec. 20, 1814, Mobile, in *Memoir of Gen. David Blackshear*, 439.

[26] John McIntosh to Peter Early, Jan. 1, 1815, Within Fifteen Miles of Chattahoochee, in *Memoir of Gen. David Blackshear*, 439.

[27] John McIntosh to David Blackshear, Jan. 9, 1815, Camp West of the Chattahoochee, in *Memoir of Gen. David Blackshear*, 441.

[28] John McIntosh to Peter Early, Jan. 1, 1815, Within Fifteen Miles of Chattahoochee, in *Memoir of Gen. David Blackshear*, 439.

[29] John McIntosh to Peter Early, Jan. 1, 1815, Within Fifteen Miles of Chattahoochee, in *Memoir of Gen. David Blackshear*, 438-39.

[30] John McIntosh to David Blackshear, Jan. 5, 1815, Fort Mitchell, in *Memoir of Gen. David Blackshear*, 437,

[31] John McIntosh to David Blackshear, Jan. 9, 1815, Camp West of the Chattahoochee, in *Memoir of Gen. David Blackshear*, 441-42.

[32] Peter Early to David Blackshear, Jan. 6, 1815, in *Memoir of Gen. David Blackshear*, 437.

[33] John McIntosh to David Blackshear, Jan. 11, 1815, West of the Chattahoochee, in *Memoir of Gen. David Blackshear*, 443.

[34] David Blackshear to John McIntosh, Jan. 11, 1815, Camp, Flint River, in *Memoir of Gen. David Blackshear*, 445.

[35] David Blackshear to John McIntosh, Jan. 14, 1815, Camp, Twelve Miles East of Flint River, in *Memoir of Gen. David Blackshear*, 447.

[36] David Blackshear to Peter Early, Jan. 14, 1815, Camp, Twelve Miles East of Flint River, in *Memoir of Gen. David Blackshear*, 447.

[37] Peter Early to David Blackshear, Jan. 10, 1815, Milledgeville, in *Memoir of Gen. David Blackshear*, 442.

[38] Peter Early to David Blackshear, Jan. 19, 1815, Milledgeville, in *Memoir of Gen. David Blackshear*, 448-49.

[39] David Blackshear to John McIntosh, January 21, 1815, Camp, Five Miles Below Hartford, in *Memoir of Gen. David Blackshear*, 450.

[40] John McIntosh to David Blackshear, Jan. 22, 1815, Fort Decatur, in *Memoir of Gen. David Blackshear*, 451.

[41] John McIntosh to David Blackshear, Jan. 23, 1815, Camp, Near Fort Decatur, in *Memoir of Gen. David Blackshear*, 451.

[42] Peter Early to David Blackshear, February 8, 1815, Executive Department, Georgia, in *Memoir of Gen. David Blackshear*, 459.

[43] McIntosh arrived at Fort Claiborne on Feb. 8; assuming he left Fort Decatur on Jan. 29, as he intended when he wrote Early on Jan. 28, the march covered eleven days. Google Maps shows the distance from the site of Fort Decatur at Milstead, Alabama, to Claiborne to be 140 miles by the most direct route.

[44] Google Maps shows the distance from Claiborne to Mobile on modern roads to be 81 miles.

[45] John McIntosh to James Winchester, Feb. 8, 1815, Fort Claiborne, in the Digital Andrew Jackson Papers at Library of Congress, Manuscript/Mixed Material, https://www.loc.gov/item/maj0049966/

[46] Andrew Jackson to John McIntosh, Feb. 22, 1815, Headquarters, 7th District, New Orleans, Digital Andrew Jackson Papers at Library of Congress, Manuscript/Mixed Material, https://www.loc.gov/item/maj00185/

[47] McIntosh was in Mobile by Feb. 22, when he discussed a prisoner exchange with a British general; John McIntosh to John Lambert, Feb. 22, 1815, Headquarters, Mobile, Digital Andrew Jackson Papers at Library of Congress, Manuscript/Mixed Material, https://www.loc.gov/item/mjm015570/

[48] John McIntosh to Andrew Jackson, March 19, 1815, Mobile, Digital Andrew Jackson Papers at Library of Congress, Manuscript/Mixed Material, https://www.loc.gov/item/maj005405/

[49] Billy Lee Atkins, "Georgians and the War of 1812" (1968), Georgia Southern College thesis for Master of Arts in History, 129-32.

[50] Owsley, *Struggle for the Gulf Borderlands*, 172-74; Joseph F. Stoltz III, *The Gulf Theater 1813-1815* (Washington: Center of Military History, United States Army, 2014), 30, 42-44.

[51] Andrew Jackson to John McIntosh, Feb. 22, 1815, Headquarters, 7th District, New Orleans, Digital Andrew Jackson Papers at Library of

Congress, Manuscript/Mixed Material, https://www.loc.gov/item/maj00185/

[52] Andrew Jackson to John McIntosh, March 13, 1815, Headquarters, 7th Military District, New Orleans, Digital Andrew Jackson Papers at Library of Congress, Manuscript/Mixed Material, https://www.loc.gov/item/maj005367/

[53] John McIntosh to Andrew Jackson, March 19, 1815, Mobile, Digital Andrew Jackson Papers at Library of Congress, Manuscript/Mixed Material, https://www.loc.gov/item/maj005405/

[54] Andrew Jackson to John McIntosh, March 13, 1815, Headquarters, 7th Military District, New Orleans, Digital Andrew Jackson Papers at Library of Congress, Manuscript/Mixed Material, https://www.loc.gov/item/maj005367/

[55] Resolution of the Georgia General Assembly approved December 16, 1815, qtd. in *Memoir of Gen. David Blackshear*, 374-75.

[56] Thomas Gamble, *Savannah Duels and Duelists,* 1923, (Savannah: Oglethorpe Press, 1997), 22. See also Cate, *Our Todays and Yesterdays*, 189.

Biographical Information

[1] Thomas Gamble, *Savannah Duels and Duelists,* 1923, (Savannah: Oglethorpe Press, 1997), 22.

[2] Margaret Davis Cate, *Our Todays and Yesterdays* (Brunswick, Ga.: Glover Brothers, revised edition, 1930), 188; Buddy Sullivan, *Early Days on the Georgia Tidewater: The Story of McIntosh County & Sapelo* (Darien: McIntosh County Board of Commissioners, 1990), 3.

[3] Mark M. Boatner III, *Encyclopedia of the American Revolution* (New York: David McKay Company, 1976), 691; *Appleton's*

Cyclopedia of American Biography v. 3 (New York, 1888, available online from Gale), 124

[4] Charles E. Bennett, *Florida's "French" Revolution 1793-1795* (Gainesville: University Presses of Florida, 1981), 83.

[5] "Mackintosh/McIntosh genealogy by Mattie R. Gladstone 1994-95," http://sites.rootsweb.com/-gamcinto/mackintosh-genealogy.html. Gladstone was a descendant of the McIntoshes who founded McIntosh County and devoted tremendous time and effort into compiling their family trees. She also edited the impressive *Cemeteries of McIntosh County, Georgia* (Darien: Lower Altamaha Historical Society, 2000).

The father of William's wife is given as "Capt. Donald McKay, wealthy Colonial merchant of St. Simons Island" in Folks Huxford, *Pioneers of Wiregrass Georgia* (Homerville, Ga., 1951), 6: 183. Page 43 of Cate's *Our Today's and Yesterdays* says Sapelo Island "was purchased by Andrew McKay, a relative of Mary Catherine McKay, who married William McIntosh."

[6] "Mackenzie Papers, Part II" ed. Albert S. Britt Jr. and Lilla M. Hawes, *Georgia Historical Quarterly* v.57 no. 1 (Spring 1973), 112.

[7] Personal communication with William S. "Billy" McIntosh Jr. of Savannah, a direct descendant of John McIntosh.

[8] Bessie Lewis, *They Called Their Town Darien* (Darien: The Darien News, 1975), 26. A photograph of the house at Fair Hope is in the Virtual Vault of the Georgia Archives in the Vanishing Georgia collection under the title "McIntosh County, ca. 1885. Fairhope Plantation. --from field notes" with the Identifier mci042-87.

[9] Sullivan, *Early Days*, 206.

[10] Sullivan, *Early Days*, 35.

[11] Gordon Burns Smith, *Morningstars of Liberty: The Revolutionary War in Georgia 1775-1783* (Milledgeville, Georgia: Boyd Publishing, 2006), 2:170.

[12] Sullivan, *Early Days*, 36-37. Captain William McIntosh was a great-grandson of Brigadier William Mackintosh of Borlum—a commander of Jacobite forces in the Risings of 1715 and 1719—through the Brigadier's natural son Benjamin. See: Iain Moncrieffe and David Hicks, *The Highland Clans,* 1967 (New York: Bramhall House, 1977), 128. John McIntosh was a great-grandson of Lachlan Mackintosh of Knocknagael—a younger brother of Brigadier William McIntosh—through his son John Mackintosh Mor, leader of the Scottish Highlanders who founded Darien. See: "Mackenzie Papers, Part II" ed. Albert S. Britt Jr. and Lilla M. Hawes, *Georgia Historical Quarterly* v.57 no. 1 (Spring 1973), 110-12; William Fraser Ross, "Family of Mackintosh of Borlum," *Clan Chattan* v. 1 no. 6 (1939), 180-90.

[13] Gordon Burns Smith, *Morningstars of Liberty: The Revolutionary War in Georgia 1775-1783* (Milledgeville, Georgia: Boyd Publishing, 2006), 2:171; James Stacy, *History and Published Records of the Midway Congregational Church, Liberty County, Georgia* (Spartanburg: The Reprint Company, 1979), 95. Stacy writes:

Col. John McIntosh, a nephew of General Lachlan McIntosh, was in command of the fort at Sunbury November 25, 1778, when he sent that laconic answer to Col. Fuser, the British officer, who had demanded its surrender, "Come and take it." It was doubtless during his stay in Liberty that his son, Col. James S. McIntosh, was born June 19, 1787, who fell mortally wounded at Molino del Rey, and died in the city of Mexico Sept. 26, 1847. [Footnote: The legislature of Georgia, a few months afterward, ordered the removal of his body, which was carried to Savannah and deposited May 18, 1848, in the tomb with his grand uncle, Major General Lachlan McIntosh.] Major Lachlan McIntosh, the brother of Col. John McIntosh, and father of Commodore James M. McIntosh, lived for awhile at Sunbury. Here his daughter, Miss Maria McIntosh, the authoress, was born in 1803, and if his son Commodore James M.

McIntosh was not born there, he was so much identified with the people that when the Georgia state legislature in 1860 requested the governor to have his remains removed from the navy yard at Pensacola, Florida, where they had been deposited, they were carried and laid beside relatives and kindred in the Midway grave yard, where they now repose. Is it saying too much, therefore, that Liberty county has an interest in, and may justly lay claim to, a part at least of the fame and valorous deeds of this remarkable family?

[14] Deposition of Josiah Tattnall, Junior, in Charles E. Bennett, *Florida's "French" Revolution 1793-1795* (Gainesville: University Presses of Florida, 1981), 141-42.

[15] Gordon Burns Smith, *History of the Georgia Militia, Vol. 1* (Milledgeville, Ga.: Boyd Publishing, 2000), 322; Cate, *Our Todays and Yesterdays*, 234.

[16] Charles E. Bennett, *Florida's "French" Revolution 1793-1795* (Gainesville: University Presses of Florida, 1981), 12-13; White, *Historical Collections of Georgia,* 551.

[17] White, *Historical Collections of Georgia,* 549.

[18] Bennett, *Florida's "French" Revolution*, 186-90.

[19] Sullivan, *Early Days*, 65.

[20] Folks Huxford, *Pioneers of Wiregrass Georgia* (Homerville, Ga., 1951), 6: 183.

[21] Cate, *Our Todays and Yesterdays*, 68.

[22] Smith, *Morningstars*, 2: 170.

[23] Cate, *Our Todays and Yesterdays*, 189; Smith, *Morningstars*, 2: 171.

The fate of John's second wife is obscure or unknown, as are the dates of John's marriage to Agnes Hillary and of her death. Charles Bennett postulates, "The widow he left was Agnes McIntosh, who had been the widow of his longtime friend Christopher Hillary of Glynn County, Georgia." *Florida's "French" Revolution 1793-1795* (Gainesville:

University Presses of Florida, 1981) 202. Bennett cites pages 187-89 of Cate's *Our Todays and Yesterdays*.

Cate writes on page 187 that Christopher Hillary died on February 18, 1796, leaving a widow and a daughter about seven years old, and, Cate continues, "Christopher Hillary's daughter, Maria, married Major William Jackson McIntosh, the son of Col. John and Swara (Swinton) McIntosh, while the widow, Agnes Hillary, married Col. John McIntosh—or, mother and daughter married father and son." Cate writes on page 189, "After the death of his first wife, Col. McIntosh married Agnes Hillary, the widow of Christopher Hillary of Glynn County, while the Colonel's son, William Jackson McIntosh, married Christopher Hillary's daughter, Maria." Cate does not specify that Agnes survived John.

P.S.: Page 171 of Smith's *Morningstars of Liberty*, volume 1, says that William Jackson McIntosh married Maria Hillary in 1808. The same page says that John McIntosh had a daughter, Marjory A. McIntosh, who died on July 15, 1806, at age four years and ten months; since Sarah died in 1799, the mother of this child would have been the widow Stevens or the widow Hillary, and John would have been about forty-six years old when the child was born. Also, the page says, John had a daughter, Anna, in 1828, two years after he died.

[24] Cate, *Our Todays and Yesterdays*, 28.

[25] Cate, *Our Todays and Yesterdays*, 243.

[26] Sullivan, *Early Days*, 216.

[27] Sullivan, *Early Days*, 72.

[28] Sullivan, *Early Days*, 140.

[29] Smith, *History of the Georgia Militia, Vol. 1*, 321-22.

[30] Revolutionary War historians say that McIntosh was born in 1755 (see, for example, Boatner, *Encyclopedia of the American Revolution*, 691), but do not give a month or day, so he would have been fifty-nine or sixty when the expedition began in November of 1814 and could have turned

sixty-one before the expedition ended in 1815. (The dates of the expedition are contained throughout *Memoir of Gen. David Blackshear*, included in *The Bench and Bar of Georgia*, ed. Stephen F. Miller (Philadelphia: J.B. Lippincott, 1858). Blackshear's memoir also is available online in the Sabin Americana series published electronically by Gale.

[31] *Register of Deaths in Savannah, Georgia* (Savannah: Georgia Historical Society, 1986), 3:42.

[32] Smith, *Morningstars*, 2: 171.

[33] Buddy Sullivan, *Early Days on the Georgia Tidewater: The Story of McIntosh County & Sapelo* (Darien: McIntosh County Board of Commissioners, 1990), 257-58.

[34] Buddy Sullivan, *Early Days on the Georgia Tidewater: The Story of McIntosh County & Sapelo* (Darien: McIntosh County Board of Commissioners, 1990), 35-36.

[35] Buddy Sullivan, *Early Days on the Georgia Tidewater: The Story of McIntosh County & Sapelo* (Darien: McIntosh County Board of Commissioners, 1990), 150.

[36] Buddy Sullivan, *Early Days on the Georgia Tidewater: The Story of McIntosh County & Sapelo* (Darien: McIntosh County Board of Commissioners, 1990), 77.

[37] Buddy Sullivan, *Early Days on the Georgia Tidewater: The Story of McIntosh County & Sapelo* (Darien: McIntosh County Board of Commissioners, 1990), 308.

[38] Buddy Sullivan, *Early Days on the Georgia Tidewater: The Story of McIntosh County & Sapelo* (Darien: McIntosh County Board of Commissioners, 1990), 514-17

[39] Buddy Sullivan, *Early Days on the Georgia Tidewater: The Story of McIntosh County & Sapelo* (Darien: McIntosh County Board of Commissioners, 1990), 213.

[40] Buddy Sullivan, *Early Days on the Georgia Tidewater: The Story of McIntosh County & Sapelo* (Darien: McIntosh County Board of Commissioners, 1990), 226.

[41] "Colonel John McIntosh laid to rest for the third time in McIntosh Co.," *The Darien News* (28 Oct. 2010), 1.

[42] Gamble, *Savannah Duels,* 22; Cate, *Our Todays and Yesterdays*, 189; reproduced in Buddy Sullivan, *Early Families of McIntosh County, Georgia* (Cedar Point, Ga.: Buddy Sullivan, 2020), 242.

A Body in Motion

[1] "Colonel John McIntosh laid to rest for the third time in McIntosh Co.," *The Darien News* (28 Oct. 2010), 17, 19.

[2] "Colonel John McIntosh laid to rest," 17.

Bibliography

Appleton's Cyclopedia of American Biography v. 3. New York, 1888, available online from Gale.

Arthur, T.S. *The History of Georgia*. Philadelphia: 1852. Retrieved online from *Sabin Americana*, Gale, Cengage Learning.

Atkins, Billy Lee. "Georgians and the War of 1812." 1968. Georgia Southern College thesis for Master of Arts in History.

Autry, Enoch. "In honor of Revolutionary War patriots." *The Sylvania Telephone* 10 October 2019: 1, 8.

Bennett, Charles E. *Florida's "French" Revolution 1793-1795*. Gainesville: University Presses of Florida, 1981.

---. *Southernmost Battlefields of the Revolution*. Bailey's Crossroads, Va.: Blair, 1970.

Blackshear, David. *Memoir of Gen. David Blackshear*, in *The Bench and Bar of Georgia*. Ed. Stephen F. Miller. Philadelphia: J.B. Lippincott, 1858. Blackshear's memoir also is available online in the Sabin Americana series published electronically by Gale.

Boatner III, Mark M. *Encyclopedia of the American Revolution*. New York: David McKay Company, 1976.

Burroughs, Wm. Berrien. "Samuel Elbert." *Men of Mark of Georgia Vol. I*. Ed. William J. Northen. Atlanta: A.B. Caldwell, 1907. 58-62.

Campbell, Archibald. *Journal of an expedition against the rebels of Georgia in North America under the orders of Archibald Campbell Esquire Lieut. Colol. of His Majesty's 71st Regimt. 1778*. Ed. Colin. Campbell. Augusta, Georgia: Richmond County Historical Society, 1981.

Cashin Jr., Edward J., and Heard Robertson. *Augusta and the American Revolution: Events in the Georgia Back Country,*

1773-1783. Augusta, Georgia: Richmond County Historical Society, 1975.

Cate, Margaret Davis. *Our Todays and Yesterdays*. Brunswick, Ga.: Glover Brothers, revised edition, 1930.

Coleman, Kenneth. *The American Revolution in Georgia 1763-1789*. Athens: University of Georgia Press, 1958.

"Colonel John McIntosh laid to rest for the third time in McIntosh Co." *The Darien News,* 28 Oct. 2010: 1+.

Coulter, E. Merton. *Georgia: A Short History*, 3rd ed. Chapel Hill: University of North Carolina Press, 1960.

Cusick, James G. *The Other War of 1812*. Athens: University of Georgia Press, 2007.

Dann, John C. *The Revolution Remembered: Eyewitness accounts of the War for Independence*. Chicago: University of Chicago Press, 1980.

Davies, K.G. *Documents of the American Revolution, 1770-1783. Vol. 17*. Shannon: Irish University Press, 1972.

Davis Jr., Robert Scott. *Encounters on a March Through Georgia in 1779: The Maps and Memorandums of John Wilson, Engineer, 71st Highland Regiment*. Sylvania, Georgia: Partridge Pond Press, 1986.

---. "Civil War in the Midst of Revolution: Community Divisions and the Battle of Briar Creek, 1779." *Georgia Historical Quarterly* 100.2 (Summer 2016): 136-59.

---. *Georgia Citizens and Soldiers of the American Revolution*. 1979. Greenville, S.C.: Southern Historical Press, 2000.

---. *Georgians in the Revolution: At Kettle Creek (Wilkes County) and Burke County*. Easley, S.C.: Southern Historical Press, 1996.

Digital Andrew Jackson Papers at Library of Congress, Manuscript/Mixed Material, https://www.loc.gov/item/majo049966/

Elliott, Daniel T. *Archaeological Investigations at Fort Morris Historic Site, Liberty County, Georgia*. Atlanta: Georgia Department of Natural Resources Parks and Historic Sites Division, 2003.

Encyclopedia of the War of 1812. Ed. David S. Heidler and Jeanne T. Heidler. Santa Barbara: ABC-CLIO, 1997.

Evans, Lawton B. *History of Georgia*. New York: American Book Company, 1898.

Fraser, Walter J. *Savannah in the Old South*. Athens: University of Georgia Press, 2003.

Gamble, Thomas. *Savannah Duels and Duelists*. 1923. Savannah: Oglethorpe Press, 1997.

Gordon, William. *The history of the rise, progress, and establishment, of the independence of the United States of America: including an account of the late war*, Vol. 3. London, printed for the author, 1788. 4 vols. Sabin Americana. Gale, Cengage Learning. University of South Carolina. 20 July 2018 <<http://galenet.galegroup.com/servlet/Sabin?af=RN&ae=CY104349274&srchtp=a&ste=14>>

Heidler, David S. "The American defeat at Briar Creek, 3 March 1779." *Georgia Historical Quarterly* 66.3 (Fall 1982): 317-31.

Heidler, David S. and Jeanne T. Heidler.

Heitman, Francis B. *Historical Register of Officers of the Continental Army during the War of the Revolution*. Washington: Rare Book Shop Publishing Company, 1914.

Howard, Joshua B., " 'Things here wear a melancholy appearance:' The American Defeat at Briar Creek." *Georgia Historical Quarterly* 88.4 (Winter 2004): 477-98.

Johnson, Daniel McDonald. *Savannah, Augusta & Brier Creek*. Allendale, S.C.: Daniel McDonald Johnson [distributed by Ingram], 2018.

Jones Jr., Charles C. *The History of Georgia*. 1883. Spartanburg, S.C.: The Reprint Company, 1969.

---. *The life and service of the honorable Major General Samuel Elbert of Georgia*. 1887. Charleston, S.C.: BiblioLife, 2011.

Lawrence, Alexander A. "General Robert Howe and the British Capture of Savannah in 1778." *Georgia Historical Quarterly* 36.4 (1952): 303-327.

Lewis, Bessie. *They Called Their Town Darien*. Darien, Georgia: The Darien News, 1975.

"Mackenzie Papers, Part II." Ed. Albert S. Britt Jr. and Lilla M. Hawes. *Georgia Historical Quarterly* v.57 no. 1 (Spring 1973), 85-145.

"Mackintosh/McIntosh genealogy by Mattie R. Gladstone 1994-95." *Rootsweb*. http://sites.rootsweb.com/-gamcinto/mackintosh-genealogy.html.

Massey, R.J. "John McIntosh." *Men of Mark of Georgia Vol. 1*. Ed. William J. Northen. Atlanta: A.B. Caldwell, 1907. 241-45.

McIlvaine, Paul. *The Dead Town of Sunbury, Georgia*. Hendersonville, N.C.: Paul McIlvaine [printed by Groves Printing Co., Asheville, N.C.], 1971.

Miscellaneous Manuscript Collection at the P.K. Yonge Library of Florida History, University of Florida, call number 00,0433, https://ufdc.ufl.edu/AA00024278/00001/thumbs

Moncrieffe, Iain, and David Hicks. *The Highland Clans*. 1967. New York: Bramhall House, 1977.

Moore, Frank. *Diary of the American Revolution from Newspapers and Original Documents Vol. 2*. 1860. New York: The New York Times & Arno Press, 1969.

Moultrie, William. *Memoirs of the American Revolution*. 1802. New York: The New York Times & Arno Press, 1968.

Murray, Patrick. "Memoir of Major Patrick Murray, Who Served in the 60th from 1770 to 1793." *The Annals of the King's Royal Rifle*

Corps. Volume 1: The Royal Americans. Lewis Butler, ed. (London: Smith, Elder & Co., 1913. 288-319.

O'Kelly, Patrick. *Nothing But Blood and Slaughter: The Revolutionary War in the Carolinas, Volume One 1771-1779.* Barbecue, N.C.: Patrick O'Kelly, 2004.

O'Riordan, Cormac A. "The 1795 Rebellion in East Florida." University of North Florida Graduate Theses and Dissertations No. 99, 1995. https://digitalcommons.unf.edu/etd/99.

Old Hickory's War: Andrew Jackson and the Quest for Empire. Baton Rouge: Louisiana State University Press, 2003.

"Order Book of Samuel Elliott, Colonel and Brigadier General in the Continental Army, October 1776 to November 1778." *Collections of the Georgia Historical Society Vol. V, Part 2.* Savannah: The Morning News Print, 1902. 5-191.

Owsley Jr., Frank Lawrence. *Struggle for the Gulf Borderlands: The Creek War and the Battle of New Orleans 1812-1815.* Gainesville: University Presses of Florida, 1981.

"Papers of James Jackson 1781-1798." Ed. Lilla M. Hawes. *Collections of the Georgia Historical Society Vol. XI.* Savannah: Georgia Historical Society, 1935.

Papers of George Washington, Revolutionary War Series. 26 vols. Ed. Dorothy Twohig, et. al. Charlottesville: University of Virginia Press, 1985.

Papers of Lachlan McIntosh. Ed. Lilla M. Hawes. Savannah: Georgia Historical Society, 1957.

Patrick, Rembert W. *Florida Fiasco: Rampant Rebels on the Georgia-Florida Border, 1810-1815.* Athens: University of Georgia Press, 1954.

Register of Deaths in Savannah, Georgia. Savannah: Georgia Historical Society, 1986.

Ross, William Fraser. "Family of Mackintosh of Borlum." *Clan Chattan* v. 1 no. 6 (1939), 180-90.

Searcy, Martha Condray. *Georgia-Florida Contest in the American Revolution, 1776-1778*. Tuscaloosa: University of Alabama Press, 1985.

Sheftall, John McKay. *Sunbury on the Medway: A Selective History of the Town, Inhabitants and Fortifications*. Atlanta: State of Georgia Department of Natural Resources Office of Planning and Research, Historic Preservation Section, 1977.

Sheftall, John McKay. *Sunbury on the Medway: A Selective History of the Town, Inhabitants and Fortifications*. Atlanta: State of Georgia Department of Natural Resources Office of Planning and Research, Historic Preservation Section, 1977.

Smith, Gordon Burns. *History of the Georgia Militia, Vol. 1: Campaigns and Generals*. Milledgeville, Georgia: Boyd Publishing, 2000.

---. *Morningstars of Liberty: The Revolutionary War in Georgia 1775-1783*. 2 vols. Milledgeville, Georgia: Boyd Publishing, 2006.

Stacy, James. *History and Published Records of the Midway Congregational Church, Liberty County, Georgia*. Spartanburg: The Reprint Company, 1979.

Stoltz III, Joseph F. *The Gulf Theater 1813-1815*. Washington: Center of Military History, United States Army, 2014.

Sullivan, Buddy. *Early Days on the Georgia Tidewater: The Story of McIntosh County & Sapelo*. Darien: McIntosh County Board of Commissioners, 1990.

---. *Early Families of McIntosh County, Georgia*. Cedar Point, Ga.: Buddy Sullivan, 2020.

White, George. *Historical Collections of Georgia*. 1855. Baltimore: Genealogical Publishing Company, 1969.

Wilson, David K. *The Southern Strategy: Britain's Conquest of South Carolina and Georgia, 1775-1780*. Columbia: University of South Carolina Press, 2005.

Wright Jr., J. Leitch. *Britain and the American Frontier, 1783-1815*. Athens: University of Georgia Press, 1975.

Index

Allen, Diego, 56, 62
Alligator Creek Bridge, 6
Amelia Island, 79, 80
Ashe, John, 24, 26, 27, 28, 29, 30, 31, 32, 33, 36
Augusta, 16, 18, 20, 22, 24, 36, 132, 133, 136, 162
Baird, James, 29
Blackshear, David, 86, 88, 89, 91, 92, 93, 94, 95, 96, 98, 99, 104, 144, 145, 147, 148, 149, 150, 152, 157, 161
Brier Creek, 19, 27, 28, 29, 30, 31, 35, 36
Burton's Ferry, 27, 30
Campbell, Archibald, 13, 14, 15, 16, 17, 18, 19, 20, 21, 22, 23, 24, 25, 26, 32, 132, 133, 134, 135, 161
Castillo de San Marcos, 58, 66, 120, 122
Clark, Elijah, 48, 69, 70, 76, 77, 79
Creek Indians, 87, 106
Cumberland Island, 7, 97, 101
Darien, 3
Early, Peter, 85, 88, 95, 96, 101
Ebenezer, 25

Elbert, Samuel, 3, 4, 5, 7, 8, 12, 14, 15, 16, 17, 19, 20, 21, 22, 24, 27, 30, 31, 32, 33, 35, 129, 130, 132, 161, 164
Elholm, Augustus George Christian, 36
Fergus, James, 28, 32, 33, 34
Fort Bowyer, 102
Fort Hawkins, 85, 88, 89, 91, 92, 96, 145, 147
Fort Morris, 2, 4, 9, 10, 11, 12, 115, 116, 163
Fort Tonyn, 6
Georgia Department of Natural Resources, 131, 136, 166
Hammond, Abner, 48, 50, 53, 56, 58, 66, 75, 76
Hammond, Samuel, 48, 49, 58, 60, 61
Havana, Cuba, 66, 67, 73, 75, 107
Hollingsworth, Timothy, 77, 78
Howard, Carlos, 49, 52, 59, 64, 65, 77
Howe, Robert, 4, 5, 6, 7, 12, 15, 16, 36, 129, 132, 164
Hudson's Ferry, 24, 25, 29

Jackson, Andrew, 85, 87, 88, 101, 102, 103, 109, 146, 150, 151, 163, 165
Jones, William, 53, 60, 62, 63, 73, 77
Lang, Richard, 49, 52, 53, 56, 57, 58, 64, 65, 66, 73, 76, 77, 78
Lincoln, Benjamin, 20, 23, 136
Maas, Luis, 78
MacAlister, Hugh, 22, 23, 32
Mackintosh, John Mor (John's grandfather), 105
Marbury, Leonard, 29
Mathews, George, 80, 82
Matthews Bluff, 28
McIntosh, Billy, 113, 114
McIntosh, John, 3, 4, 3, 6, 8, 10, 11, 18, 19, 24, 27, 32, 36, 38, 39, 41, 42, 43, 44, 45, 47, 48, 49, 50, 51, 52, 68, 69, 70, 71, 76, 78, 80, 82, 85, 86, 87, 105, 106, 107, 108, 109, 110, 113, 114, 115, 117, 118, 120, 123, 124, 127, 129, 130, 131, 136, 137, 141, 143, 144, 145, 146, 147, 148, 149, 150, 151, 152, 153, 154, 155, 156, 157, 158, 159, 162, 164, 167
McIntosh, John Houstoun (John's cousin), 80
McIntosh, Lachlan (John's uncle), 106

McIntosh, Roderick, 11, 12, 131
McIntosh, Sarah, 36, 41, 47, 50, 59, 67, 68, 70, 71, 73, 74, 75, 107, 108, 137, 156
McIntosh, William (British captain), 106, 153
McIntosh, William (Creek Indian leader), 87, 146
McIntosh, William (John's brother), 52, 68
McIntosh, William (John's father), 38, 105
McIntosh, William (John's son), 74
Miller Bridge, 27, 32
Mitchell, David B., 81, 82
Mobile, Alabama, 85, 92, 94, 99, 102
Moultrie, William, 34, 36, 134, 135, 136, 165
New Orleans, 87, 92, 94, 102, 146, 150, 151, 165
Paris's Mill, 26, 28, 29
Plowden, William, 55, 56, 57, 58, 73, 76, 77
Prevost, Augustine, 18, 25, 35
Prevost, James Mark, 25, 26, 29, 31
Purrysburg, 23, 26, 28, 34
Quesada, Juan Nepomuceno de, 54, 55, 56, 60, 71, 78
Red Sticks, 87, 90, 93
Ross, Francis, 28, 29
San Nicolas, 77, 78, 79, 107

Savannah, 2, 12, 14, 15, 16, 18, 19, 22, 23, 24, 25, 26, 27, 28, 29, 30, 31, 33, 35, 47, 48, 59, 69, 87, 101, 104, 105, 109, 110, 113, 114, 127, 129, 131, 132, 136, 137, 143, 144, 145, 152, 153, 154, 157, 158, 163, 164, 165, 166

Savannah River, 12, 14, 15, 20, 22, 23, 27, 28, 29, 30, 31, 33, 35

Seventy-first Regiment, 13, 22, 29, 31

Slavery, 41, 42, 43, 109, 110

Spalding, Margery McIntosh (John's sister), 106

St. Augustine, 8, 10, 12, 42, 43, 45, 49, 50, 52, 53, 54, 55, 58, 60, 71, 73, 79, 80, 82, 83, 143

St. Johns district, 41, 45, 46, 55, 58

St. Johns River, 7, 41, 43, 53, 55, 56, 59, 62, 76, 77, 107

St. Simons Island, 3, 79, 101, 108, 153

Sumter, Thomas, 36

Sunbury, 4, 8, 11, 18, 36, 131, 132, 136, 166

Wagnon, John Peter, 50, 51, 52, 54, 55, 56, 57, 58, 61, 62, 63, 67, 73, 77

War of 1812, 3, 5, 85, 87, 106, 109, 116, 142, 143, 146, 147, 151, 161, 162, 163

Washington, George, 4, 49, 133, 141, 166

Winchester, James, 92, 95, 100, 101, 102

www.ingramcontent.com/pod-product-compliance
Lightning Source LLC
Chambersburg PA
CBHW072007290426
44109CB00018B/2159